Week-end Painter

Week-end Painter

by LAURENCE V. BURTON

Whittlesey House NEW YORK · TORONTO

McGRAW-HILL BOOK COMPANY, INC.

ND
1260
B 55

PUBLISHED BY WHITTLESEY HOUSE

A division of the McGraw-Hill Book Company, Inc.

Printed in the United States of America

29247

THIS VOLUME IS DEDICATED TO
BUSY MEN AND WOMEN WHO WOULD
LIKE TO LEARN HOW TO PAINT IN OILS YET
HAVE ONLY WEEK ENDS FREE TO DEVOTE TO
THIS FASCINATING HOBBY

Preface

THIS LITTLE volume is a partial answer to the question once hurled at me by a total stranger:

"Say, how do you get started painting? What do you need to buy? And what do you do when you get it?"

Not so many years ago I, too, wanted that same information and wondered how to get it. My physician had ordered me to take up a hobby that would be so absorbing I could forget all about business. In fact, he hinted none too gently that, unless I rode a hobby hard, I might as well wind up my affairs and purchase a very small plot of ground.

Painting became that hobby.

Painting pictures always had a fascination for me, but how did one get started? How did one learn to paint? I bought quantities of books and studied voraciously. Some of my books, which now fill an entire bookcase, have been read and reread. Others have proved to be of very little help. Apparently I was seeking something that was not in the printed page. This volume, therefore, is my own version of the craftsmanship of landscape painting in oils. It is the sort of book I would gladly have purchased when I began painting for it tries to tell what I wanted to know but could not learn from the available books about painting. Though it consists of fragments gleaned here and there, much of it is the result of my own experimentation.

It was fortunate that I had a neighbor who also wanted to take up painting. We struggled along, unaided, for years. Both of us were too busy to attend an art school. Furthermore, it did not seem quite appropriate for two grayheads to join a class of teen-agers. Nevertheless we did attend a few night classes for adults, but it was in another town, and my business took me all over the country. After a few rather widely separated sessions I was so far behind the rest of the class that the only sensible thing was to drop out.

To this extent I received a trifling bit of instruction—indoors and at night—and we painted by the light of ordinary incandescent lights. Most of the progress I have been able to make in the craftsmanship of painting has been without the aid of formal instruction. Yet it would be inaccurate to say that I am wholly self-taught. We learn from all manner of sources and judging from my brief contact with art classes, I should say that we learn more from our fellow students than from an instructor no matter how conscientious he may be. This is true if for no other reason than that his time is spread over some forty students.

The principal controlling factor in our education in any subject is our desire to learn. As Robert Henri put it in *The Art Spirit*, "No knowledge is so easily found as when it is needed."

One who really desires to learn to paint can learn by doing. I fondly believe, however, that in the absence of a competent instructor, you will proceed more rapidly as a result of what I have assembled in this volume.

It has been necessary for me to make several basic assumptions about the persons for whom this book has been written. Many would-be week-end or Sunday painters have questioned me so much that I assume:

1. You are a successful business man or woman, too old or too busy to attend an art school.

2. You can afford to buy the equipment needed without

starting an argument about the state of the family exchequer.

3. You have poise enough to brush aside any jokes about going arty.

4. You enjoy going to art exhibits and perhaps you own a few paintings.

5. You are, above all, a perfectionist. You believe that what is worth doing at all is worth trying to do well.

Painting is a form of relaxation that will take you out in the open air and sunlight, give you a moderate amount of exercise, will get you to bed on time, will open up a whole new world the existence of which you probably never even suspected. It will contribute to your health and happiness and to next week's business efficiency, and will give you the wholesome joy of creating something.

Should a student in a formal art course study this volume and derive any benefit from it I should be highly gratified—also surprised. For this book is not intended for anything but an otherwise unavoidable substitute for competent instruction, something I have longed for but missed. Rather it is the summation of twelve years of solo effort by trial and error to learn the craftsmanship or techniques of oil painting.

Should this book really prove to be as helpful to others as I hope it will, I will appreciate your sending to the publisher any questions that should have been answered by the text. If a need to revise the text should ever arise, your concrete suggestions will serve as an admirable guide for its improvement.

Some of my friends who read this volume in manuscript objected to the logical sequence of the chapters on the ground that the chap who wants to start painting immediately will want to read the part on painting first. They believe he might be discouraged if he has to wade through a lot of preliminary explanations.

To this criticism there is only one possible answer: It's your book. Anyone who wants to start reading at page 120 is at liberty to do so. There is no rule to compel anyone to read any special chapter or to read them in any special sequence.

My suggestion is that you start reading wherever you find it most interesting. Then go to any other place in the book where you believe you will find help. If Chapter XII appeals to you most, by all means read it first. Then skip around to your heart's content. That's the way I read most of the art books in my collection. The only reason for the logical sequence of the chapters is to help you when you are seeking information on some particular phase of painting. If there is some semblance of order in the presentation, you may locate what you are after more quickly.

LAURENCE V. BURTON

Contents

ONE

Why *You* Should Paint

SELDOM WILL you find a person who has looked upon a satisfying painting or a good reproduction of a painting without having experienced a secret desire to be able to do the same sort of thing. And sometimes it does not require even a very good picture to arouse this desire. Yet most people regard painting as something that only the gifted few can do, little realizing that anyone can learn to paint pictures be they good, bad, or indifferent in quality. It takes only a little equipment and patience, plus the real desire to paint.

If you are one who "doodles" on a sheet of paper when telephoning, or if you experience even a minor thrill at the sight of a cottage with flowers growing in the front yard, or if you enjoy a long look at the sunset, or if you get a kick out of the sight of a comely young lady in gayly colored clothes, or if you arrange and rearrange your furniture in order to make your home look more attractive, you are the kind of person who will enjoy painting. It really is fun, right from the start.

Some folks have asked me why I go to the effort of painting a picture when all I really need to do is buy some Kodachrome film for my camera, press the button, and let the Eastman Kodak Company do the rest? As a matter of fact, I have done just that on hundreds of occasions when my time was too short for even the quickest sort of a water color, let alone a more careful sketch in oils.

Yet I have never made a Kodachrome shot that would recreate my sensations when visiting the original scene. (And, alas, my Kodachromes fade in a few years.) A camera shot is a factual record of a scene. At best there is little of your own creative effort in it.

As one chap puts it, an artist is a commentator, not a reporter. The artist singles out a few essentials for the creation of the picture he sees when gazing on a scene. The camera can be used in somewhat the same manner when in the hands of an expert, but the photographer usually has to accomplish his selection by getting very close to his subject so as to exclude as many nonessentials as possible. The painter, on the other hand, has far more ease and latitude because he can choose the essentials and disregard all else. Furthermore, he can place his essentials exactly where he wants them. The camera cannot often do that. I do not decry the camera; I own five of them. But photography is not the same medium as painting. It has a totally different application.

One paints because he wants to paint, because he enjoys it, whether he does it as a hobby or as a means of livelihood. And, whether painting be his avocation or vocation, he paints interestingly if he has something to say, if he has an interesting mind, and uninterestingly if he has a commonplace mind. He paints well if he has mastered the craftsmanship of painting and poorly if he has not acquired the skills of the craft. As one artist once told me, painting is both a trade and a profession. Yet a craft or trade cannot be learned by reading and inspection alone. Only actual practice can make craftsmanship a part of your possessions.

To anyone who may be timid about painting in public, let me say that those who know nothing about painting are invariably great admirers of any sort of artistic endeavor while those who really know all about painting will seldom stop and will never suggest anything to you. In fact, the accomplished artist will not even look at your work without a specific request. There have been only two instances in twelve years where a

Plate I. BARNYARD

After ten years of self-teaching this imaginary picture was created. Only the barn, a pi
of gravel instead of a strawstack, the road, and the hedge existed in the original subjec
In painting, you create the picture you want to see: it seldom exists in nature.

passer-by who really knew anything about painting has spoken to me.

If timidity deters you from painting, you have nothing to fear, no comments to embarrass, from anyone but yourself.

~~~~~~

TWO

Water Color, Pastels, or Oils—Which?

IF YOU are going to paint pictures, you will need to outfit yourself with the tools of the trade. Your first decision, therefore, must be what medium to use: water color, oils, or pastels. In giving you the results of my own experience I am not trying to influence your choice. This book, however, is about oil painting.

My first essays into the field of art were made with some school kids' crayons. There were only six colors in the set. Their limitations were soon obvious: I needed more colors, but where could I get them? This led me to the discovery of pastels, and soon I acquired enough pastel crayons to fill a couple of shoe boxes. It was then that I discovered that not all pastels are what the ladies mean when they speak of "pastel colors," for some of mine were intensely strong. The colors were anything but "soft." In those days I didn't have enough sense to buy a book on the subject of pastel painting (really, drawing with colored chalk), but it did not take me more than a few months to realize that pastel colors cannot be mixed in the same manner as paints. Either you have the correct color in a single crayon, or you don't. And, if you don't, nothing can be done about it.

Furthermore, the dust from the crayons made me sneeze at most inopportune times. Several of my pictures were badly sneezed upon and ruined.

Water color then seemed to me to be the proper medium, so I put the pastels away and bought water colors, paper, and brushes. Things went far better now, but in time I discovered that water color also has its limitations. If one knows how to

4

paint and can put every color on the paper correctly the first time the brush touches it, then water color is highly satisfactory. But the beginner is seldom right the first time and makes innumerable mistakes he would like to correct. While it is possible to make a few corrections in water-color painting, the results are usually bad. The more one tries to correct mistakes, the muddier the colors become.

Furthermore, painting in water color seems to be a sort of subtractive process. One starts with the clean paper, which is as light as it is possible to get, and from that maximum lightness one works downward toward darkness. The more color one puts on, the darker the color becomes.

Oils, on the other hand, are additive. One puts on lighter paint to go up the scale of lightness or darker paint to go down the scale toward darkness. It soon became obvious to me that much more freedom of action is possible in oil painting than in any other medium. So I put aside the water colors and bought an oil kit. After some years of experience, I am of the opinion that I would now be much farther along if I had started with oils in the first place; and, of course, still farther along the road to painting in the way I should like to paint if I had also received plenty of competent instruction and criticism.

Water color is really more difficult to master than oil painting. Therefore, in my humble judgment, the beginner will do better to start with oils as long as he wants to work in color. Later, after he has learned how to paint with oils, he can go to water colors or pastels with greater chances of success.

But water color does have practical advantages over oils for the week-end painter. The equipment is less bulky and is considerably lighter to carry. The finished pictures take up less space. Spilled water color is easier to clean up than oil paints. And, as a rule, it does not take as much time to complete a sketch in water color. When you are through you can pack up and be ready to go home more quickly than you can when using an oil kit.

It is often said that a water color should be completed in an hour after starting to paint. But an oil painting of comparable size can also be done quickly. Plate II, a 12- by 16-inch panel, required a little less than an hour to do. *The Clam Digger* (Plate III), on the other hand, represents well over a hundred hours of work, but it is much larger, being 22 by 30. If your time is extremely limited you will probably get more color on the painted surface by using water color, but unless you are very good you may not be satisfied with the results.

The disadvantages of water-color painting are also numerous. The paper must lie flat, or the water will run and cause you no end of grief. This means that you must either put your paper on the ground to paint, or you must carry a little table or an easel especially designed for water colors *and* a chair or stool. Eliot O'Hara, in his book *Making Watercolor Behave*, recommends kneeling over the paper placed on the ground when painting. This is probably satisfactory to a lean individual like Mr. O'Hara, but it is not my idea of having a good time. It is much more satisfactory and more conducive to good work to be able to stand up to the job. This gives oils the advantage.

Water must evaporate from a water color while it is being painted. There are frequent pauses for drying before going on with the next step. If the relative humidity of the atmosphere is very high, the water on the paper dries with exasperating slowness. You may become impatient with the long delays and resume painting too soon, with the result that the colors run into each other. I have found that when the humidity is above 95 per cent, it is useless to try to paint in water color at all.

After balancing the advantages and disadvantages of the various mediums for the beginner, it is my opinion that he will do best to begin working with oil paints. After he has made considerable progress, it will then be possible for him to use another medium with greater certainty of progress. I quite agree with John Carlson's statement that water color is a master's medium.

~~~~~~

THREE

Equipment and Materials for Oil Painting

Now that you have decided to try your hand at oil painting, you will need some equipment. To be sure, you can get by with a few tubes of color, one brush, an old pie tin for a palette, and a canvas panel nailed to the barn. A really good artist could paint a fairly good picture with such inadequate equipment. But you won't get much pleasure out of painting if you don't have most of the necessary tools.

Almost any book on painting will give you detailed instructions on what to buy. But they seldom tell you what *quality* to buy. My advice is to get the best. It's cheaper in the long run.

Some of the larger artists'-supply stores in big cities provide catalogs of their equipment and supplies. You may save yourself time by consulting such literature before actually shopping.

You will want a paintbox for either 12-by-16- or 16-by-20-inch canvas panels. Don't buy a cheap one! Sometimes before the war you could find a 12-by-16-inch box for sale as low as $2.75. Shun this kind of purchase. The wood is soft, the screws or nails come loose, the hinges come off, the corners come unglued, and the whole thing may fall apart in a couple of years. It is far better to buy the most expensive hardwood or metal box you can find, metal lined, with brass screws and a reinforced leather handle. But make sure that the dimensions are accurate and that the canvas panels actually fit into the slots in the lid.

Panels should slip into the lid with ease. If a panel has to be bowed to get it in, you are in for all sorts of unhappiness.

You will also want an easel. Here again my advice, based on

8

sad experience, is to get the best that money will buy. Be sure to get hardwood, with an aluminum head frame (if you can find one), or all aluminum. A softwood easel is light to carry, but its screws loosen and pull out, and it soon grows wobbly. You'll curse it in time and then buy the one you should have had in the first place.

When you buy an easel, insist on finding out all about how it works. Frequently you'll have to experiment, but do so before you buy the easel or leave the store. Put in panels of various sizes, also stretched canvases. Some easels are weird contraptions that you'll be sorry to own. The time to learn about them is before, not after, they are paid for.

I have never owned one of those combination box-easels. But an artist of my acquaintance uses one and likes it.

Never buy a tiny easel at which you must sit down to work. You can't do a good oil painting sitting down—or stooping down to a diminutive easel. In my experience, oil painting is a standing-up job—no fooling. Furthermore, those tiny easels tip over or blow over too easily. It's very disheartening to have a wet painting blow over "butter side down"—which is the way they always fall—and have to spend the next hour picking leaves and dirt from a picture.

Brushes are another item where the best is none too good. The bristles of cheap brushes break off, and the handles soon become loose and wobbly. I prefer Mussini or Rembrandt brushes when I can get them. There are other good makes, however. A few good brushes are to be preferred to a few dozen cheap ones.

You'll want one large flat bristle brush, about ¾ inch wide, a couple of ½-inch brushes, and a half dozen each of the smaller ones. Two small round brushes, No. 2 and No. 3, are useful.

Brushes come in long and short bristles, and you will use whichever you find most effective. My experience is that short bristles are the most satisfactory for my own work, probably because I have a "heavy touch."

After you have painted awhile you will need some Russian-sable brushes, but you can put off buying these for several years. They cost real money and are easily ruined by improper use or improper care. When you do buy them the same rule holds: get the best that money will buy, *and take proper care of them!*

Other items of equipment you will need are the following:

Palette. Every paintbox usually has a rectangular palette. This is plenty good enough to last for years. The palette is equipped with a thumb hole, and you hold it in the left hand with the left thumb inserted through the hole. A small palette is easy to hold, but when you use a large rectangular palette it may give you paralysis of the thumb in a short time. My 16-by-20-inch palette becomes an unbearable burden in an hour. In addition to holding the palette, you have to hold several brushes and a towel or paint cloth for cleaning brushes; it's too much of a chore to hold them all. I have solved the problem by carrying along a water-color easel with a tilting top, upon which I place my palette, making it a sort of portable painting table (see Fig. 13, between pages 92 and 93). By freeing yourself of vexations in this way, you can do a much better picture. There is no avoiding the fact that your picture is a direct reflection of your mental attitude while you are painting.

The curved palette is for studio use by an accomplished artist. However, for studio painting, most artists who make a living at it seem to prefer a painting table. This is usually a table with a glass top placed over a piece of clean canvas. One commercial artist uses an enamel-topped kitchen table. Other artists have special tables or cabinets made to the appropriate height to serve as painting tables.

Palette Knife. This is a tool with which to do most of your mixing of color. A straight-bladed spatula is a poor substitute for the trowel-type (offset-from-the-handle) palette knife. You can also paint with it in a technique called "knifework."

Tube Colors. You will want a variety of colors, even at the beginning. If you have a box that is 12 by 16 inches or larger, buy "studio-sized" tubes. Get artist's colors, not student's colors, which are often dishearteningly diluted with fillers. The following should be purchased at the outset (see also Chap. V, "Paints and How to Use Them"):

White (1-pound tube: Zinc White, Perma Alba, or Titanium White)
Payne's Gray
Cadmium Yellow, Light
Cadmium Orange, Medium
Yellow Ochre
Raw Sienna

Burnt Sienna
Raw Umber
Burnt Umber
Alizarin Crimson
Cobalt Blue, Dark
French Ultramarine
Winsor Blue or Prussian Blue

Finder. This is a piece of really stiff cardboard, with a rectangular hole cut in its center, having the same proportions as the canvas on which you are to paint. Use it to help you pick out the subject matter in a landscape that will give you good pictorial composition. Make it yourself.

Towel. An old bath towel makes an excellent paint rag for wiping hands and brushes. I also take paper towels along for removing the bulk of the paint from my brushes.

Paint Cups. These are small tin cups with clips on the bottom that clip them onto the edge of the palette. I use a large one for turpentine and a small one for the medium. Don't buy them fastened together in pairs, because if you want to dump one of them you are sure to lose the contents of the other.

Turpentine. Buy a quart can of the best grade of turpentine from a store selling house paints. Keep it at home.

Turpentine Can. Buy a small, rectangular, flat can with a screw top (be sure the top has a good liner) from an artists'-supply store to hold a small quantity of turpentine. Be sure it will fit somewhere into your box.

Medium Can. Buy a smaller can to carry your painting medium. Be sure you are able to fit it *and* the turpentine can into your paintbox—along with all the rest of your equipment.

Painting Medium. This is a fluid to mix with oil paints to make them more free-flowing. Some artists never use a medium; others invariably use one. You can buy the medium already mixed, or you can mix your own. The mixture I use is my own modification of the one recommended by John Carlson:

> 2 parts oil of copal (not picture copal)
> 1 part stand oil (thickened linseed oil)
> 1 part raw linseed oil

Scraper. A smooth-edged, curved grapefruit knife is a better scraper than a palette knife to remove the wet paint from a canvas when you have made an error. This is a hardware-store purchase.

Pencil or Charcoal. This is for drawing on the canvas when you start to compose a picture. Some folks prefer charcoal, but I prefer a No.-2 pencil.

Eraser. If you use charcoal, you will want a kneaded rubber eraser. If you prefer to use a pencil, you will need an artist's gum eraser.

Canvas Panels. Most of your painting will be done on canvas panels. These are made of heavy cardboard with sized canvas glued to it. The board acts as a stretcher to hold the canvas. Panels come in a variety of sizes. Buy a dozen of the size that fits your paintbox cover. Be sure that the measurements are true. If too long, the panels may not fit into the slots in the cover of your paintbox; or, if too short, they may fall out. After you have gained a little experience you will want to paint on other sizes at home. At the present time I have a dozen or so each of fresh panels in sizes 8 by 10, 12 by 16, 16 by 20, and 20 by 24 inches.

Stretched Canvas.   You can put off purchasing a stretched canvas for a year or so, but some day you will want to use one. This is a piece of sized canvas stretched on a demountable frame made of four mortised strips of wood. Be sure to get the wooden wedges with which to stretch, or "key," the canvas to make it taut. For small pictures, up to 16 by 20, you will find canvas panels entirely satisfactory. For pictures larger than 16 by 20 you will probably prefer stretched canvases, but you will find they are more suitable for work at home than out of doors.

Because of the shortage of textiles you may have to take whatever weave you can get. But the time will come when you will want coarse, medium, or fine-weave canvases for different purposes.

Other Materials.   You can paint—after a fashion—with oil colors on almost any sort of surface, even paper or cardboard. (I have seen this done by artists who were making very rapid sketches.) Special wooden panels were once available and may again come back into use.

Masonite is a material that finds favor with some artists. It is heavy, which is a drawback, but it can be cut to almost any usable size. It is used in building and can be purchased in large sheets from almost any lumber dealer. One side is smooth, the other rough. Most artists prefer the rough side. It must be prepared, however, by first coating the side to be used with a light paint. Casein White—a water paint—seems to be wholly satisfactory for this purpose.

Masonite may be too thick to carry in your paintbox unless you have the box specially constructed. It is heavy to carry, but it does not warp, chip, or break unless it is treated with extreme roughness.

This completes the list of things you will need at the outset. There are, however, a few other remarks that are appropriate here.

Umbrella. Sometimes when you are out painting there is no shade where you want to work. To work with direct sunlight falling on your canvas is disastrous. Your picture will turn out wholly unsatisfactory. The only remedy is an umbrella. An artist's umbrella is an extra-large umbrella with a long shaft equipped with a stake to drive into the ground so that it will stand by itself and throw shade on the canvas. One of my painting companions uses a beach umbrella. I have a fancy contraption that is forever twisting with the wind; I wish I had back the $15 it cost me. John Carlson's book says he uses an ordinary black umbrella held in his left hand while painting. I have never tried this.

Stools or Chairs. Some folks prefer to paint sitting down. So do I, if I am doing a water color. But to my way of thinking you can't paint a good picture in oils and sit down. Time was when I included a comfortable folding chair in my equipment, but I abandoned it about seven years ago. You stand up to do a good picture in oils.

Usually I take my annual holiday in the autumn and paint for two solid weeks. During all this time I seldom sit down during the daylight except for meals. Naturally it's hard on the feet of an office worker, but with proper foot exercises your arches can be strengthened until you can stand all day with no effort.

FOUR

How to Find Your Way in Color

Since color is principally what makes painting interesting, you will want to understand what color is and how to control it. Even a modest technical knowledge of color and its three dimensions will help you make more rapid progress as you learn to paint.

Nothing has been of greater help to me than this knowledge. In art schools it is called "color theory." It teaches you how to make colors do what you want them to do, how to make objects appear to recede into the distance, or how to make them come closer. It also teaches you how to create a mood in a picture—sunshine or drabness—and how to give shape to objects.

There are many ways of considering color. The artist's understanding of color is not to be confused with the studies made by physiologists, psychologists, physicists, chemists, colorists, designers, and paint and ink manufacturers. Some deal with human vision, others with colored light, and others with pigments. In painting we are concerned principally with pigments—the things that give color to paint.

Everything I shall say about color is in terms of the Munsell Color System, devised some years ago by the late Albert H. Munsell. Although there are other methods of identifying color, I particularly like this one. Munsell developed the idea that color has three dimensions: Hue, Value, and Chroma. And, unlike some others, his system allows for the discovery of new pigments that are different from any we know today. In this respect it occupies a place roughly comparable to the Periodic Table of the chemist in which there were once

15

blank spaces for predictable, though undiscovered, elements.

Although the general public may not be aware of it, new colors are being discovered from time to time. Perhaps I should say that new *pigments* are being discovered, for many of us have seen colors that have no counterparts in the form of pigments. Most of these new pigments are the products of research in the field of synthetic organic chemistry. A few of the newly discovered pigments are useful, but most of them are too unstable and fugitive (subject to fading) to be of enduring value to artists. The artist must use colors that do not fade or change; otherwise his picture will change with the passage of time. Some pictures actually do change, but not always because of fading of colors. More often this is due to color changes in vehicles or varnishes or to the accumulation of plain ordinary dirt.

Not many years ago I had occasion to call on the DuPont Finishes Dept. in connection with my business and was given a look into their color book. There I saw many swatches of color that were new and comparatively unknown. By this I mean pigments that, up to the time of their discovery, nobody had ever seen before. Until Perkin discovered the synthetic organic dye we know now as "Mauve," nobody had ever seen that color before—at least as a pigment. Recently a new color known as "Thioviolet" has come on the market as an artist's color.

In the Munsell System, the future existence of both of these colors and a host of others as well is allowed for. To understand this System, I suggest that you read Munsell's book called *A Color Notation*. You will also find the System admirably described in a condensed form in "A Practical Description of the Munsell Color System," by T. M. Cleland, published in 1937 by the Munsell Color Company of Baltimore, Maryland. The company has graciously permitted me to quote extensively from Mr. Cleland's lucid essay and to reproduce some of his diagrams:

"The first essential to the application of the Munsell Color System is a clear understanding of the three dimensions of color, and once having grasped the simple logic of these, the practical advantages of the system will be manifest. The reader should be warned at the outset against that fear of scientific perplexity which is ever present in the lay mind. The three dimensions of color are not involved in the mysteries of higher mathematics. There is nothing about them which should not be as readily comprehended by the average reader as the three dimensions of a box, or any other form which can be felt or seen. We have been unaccustomed to regarding color with any sense of order and it is this fact, rather than any complexity inherent in the idea itself, which will be the source of whatever difficulty may be encountered by the reader, who faces this conception of color for the first time.

"The idea of the three dimensions of color can be expressed thus:

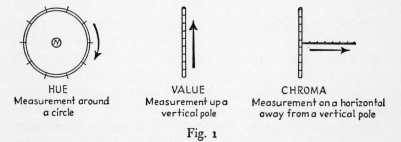

HUE
Measurement around
a circle

VALUE
Measurement up a
vertical pole

CHROMA
Measurement on a horizontal
away from a vertical pole

Fig. 1

"With these three simple directions of measurement well in mind, there need be little confusion for even the least scientific mind in comprehending what is meant by color 'measurement.' In considering further the qualities of color, which are expressed by these three dimensions known as Hue, Value, and Chroma, we will take each one of them separately in the order in which they are written, trusting that having done so we may pass to the subject of color balance or harmony and its application to everyday practice, equipped with a clear understanding of how it may be measured and noted.

I. Hue

"The first dimension is defined by Mr. A. H. Munsell as 'the quality by which we distinguish one color from another, as a red from a yellow, a green, a blue, or a purple,' but this dimension does not tell us whether the color is dark or light, or strong or weak. It merely refers to some point in the spectrum of all colors, such as we have seen in the reflection of sunlight through a prism. Let us suppose now that we had such a spectrum cast by a prism, or a section taken out of a rainbow. We know it to be a scientific fact that it contains all possible Hues, merging by indistinguishable degrees, one into the other, but always in a fixed order. Now let us imagine that we have such a spectrum fixed or printed on a band of paper, and that it begins at one

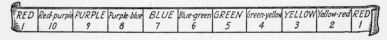

Fig. 2

end with red and going through all possible Hues, it arrives back at red again at the other end. The hues are unevenly divided and they merge one into the other by indistinguishable degrees. But still preserving the order of these Hues, let us divide them into equal steps as we do a ruler into inches by selecting certain colors familiar to us in everyday use—red, yellow, green, blue, and purple. These we will call the Principal Hues, but between each of them we will make another division where each merges into the other. These we will call yellow-red, green-yellow, blue-green, purple-blue, and red-purple and they will be known as Intermediate Hues, because they are Intermediate or halfway between the Principal Hues. Thus we shall have ten divisions upon our band. . . . Now if we bend this band around into a circular hoop, so that the red at one end meets and laps the red at the other end, we have a perfect scale of Hue in the circular form in which we shall always consider it. So it is that when we state the first dimension

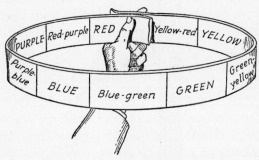

Fig. 3

of a color we are merely referring to its position on this circle of hues. In writing a color formula this first dimension is expressed by the initial letter of the Hue—R for red, which is a Principal Hue, and B-G for blue-green which is an Intermediate Hue. . . .

II. VALUE

"This is the second dimension and is possibly the simplest to understand. It is, according to Mr. Munsell's definition, 'the quality by which we distinguish a light color from a dark one.' We noted that the first dimension did not tell us whether a color was light or dark. It told us, for example, that it was red and not green, but we know that there may be light red and dark red, and it is the function of this dimension of Value to tell us how light or how dark a given color may be. For this purpose we shall need a scale of Value, which we may conceive as a vertical pole, or axis to our circle of Hues, black at the lower end, representing total absence of light, and white at the top, representing pure light, and between these a number of

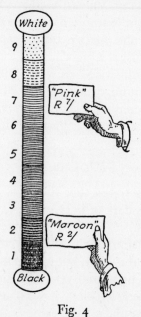

Fig. 4

divisions of gray, regularly graded between black and white. . . . Since pure black is unattainable, we will call that 0 and begin our scale with the darkest gray as 1, numbering the steps up to 9, which is the lightest gray. Pure white, which is also unattainable, we will call 10. In the practical use of the scale of Value, therefore, we shall have but nine steps and the middle one of these will be 5—what is referred to as Middle Value. These steps of Value have been scientifically measured and registered by means of an instrument known as a photometer. In writing a color formula we express this dimension of Value by a numeral, which denotes at what step upon the scale of Value this color falls. This numeral is written above a line, as B6/ for example, by which we mean that this particular blue, regardless of its other qualities, is as light or as dark as the sixth step upon the scale of Value. A color such as is commonly called 'maroon' is an example of a red which is *low in value*, because it is dark, and what is called 'pink' is a red which is *high in Value* because it is light.

"Now having familiarized ourselves with these two dimensions, and understanding what qualities of a color they express, we may proceed to consider the third dimension, without which our description of any given color is incomplete.

III. Chroma

"When we have stated that the color is blue or yellow or green and that it is dark or light, we have indicated two of its important qualities—its Hue and its Value—but we have by no means described it completely. We may say of an emerald that it is green and that it is light, but we can say that certain grapes are green and also light, and yet there is a decided difference between their respective colors, if we place them side by side. Both may be green and of the same Value of light, but the emerald is *strong* in color and the grape is *weak* in color or *grayer*. It is this difference which is measured on the dimension of Chroma. The scale of Value may be referred to in the convenient and easily understood form of a vertical pole, which represents a neutral axis to all the circle of Hues and is, itself, of no color, but is pure gray. Around this pole we may place our band representing the scale of Hue and then if we imagine any one of these hues on the circumference of the band to grow in-

ward toward the gray pole in the center, growing grayer or
weaker in color strength until it reaches this center pole and
loses its color entirely, we have grasped the idea of the dimension known as Chroma. By dividing this into regular measured
steps, we have a scale upon which the strength of color may be
measured. This dimension of Chroma is written in a color

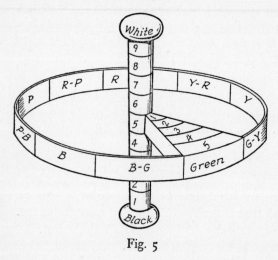

Fig. 5

formula by means of a numeral *below* a line, which denotes the
step upon the Chroma scale at which it falls, thus /5, /8, /9,
etc.

"Needless to say, all of the Hues may be thus measured on
this dimension at right angles to the vertical pole and grading
from gray, step by step away from the pole to greater and
greater strength of color.

"Mr. Munsell in his book *A Color Notation*, refers to 'the
Color Sphere.' * This is a general form which aids the orderly

* The Munsell Color Sphere is a globe, the north pole of which represents
white, the south pole black, and the axis made up of a sequence of grays ex-
tending from white to black. Around the equator is a band of Hues whose Value

consideration of color and within which all color balances, as will be shown later; but in the actual measurement of pigment colors, such as we use in printing or painting, all of the paths of Chroma would not be of the same length nor would they all be comprised within a Sphere. Certain of them would extend to points outside of it. Nor would all of the paths of Chroma reach their greatest length at the equator of the Sphere, that is the level of Middle Value. There are two reasons governing

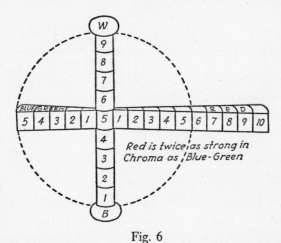

Fig. 6

this which it is important to understand: first, *colors differ by nature in their Chroma strength, some being much more powerful than others.* The strongest red pigment used, for example, is twice as powerful as the strongest blue-green pigment and will require a correspondingly greater number of steps on a longer path to reach gray. The Chroma path of red is the longest and extends far outside the sphere, being ten measured

is 5/ and Chroma /5. Above the equator are bands of Hues of successively higher Value, while below it are bands of successively lower Value. Upon rotating the Sphere each band of Hues turns to gray. (Condensed from A *Color Notation,* Seventh Edition, 1927, page 19.)

steps from the neutral pole; * while blue-green is the shortest, being only five steps. The Sphere is limited in size to this shortest axis for reasons which will appear when we take up the question of balance or harmony of color. The second reason is: *that all colors do not reach their maximum Chroma strength at the same level of Value.* It can be readily comprehended, for example, that the strongest yellow pigment is by nature much

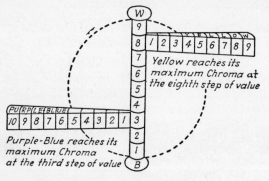

Fig. 7

lighter, or higher in Value, than the strongest blue pigment and, therefore, that the complete Chroma paths of these two colors will touch the neutral pole at different levels.

"Thus it is evident that a complete image of all pigment colors cannot be comprised within the sphere; and we are led to seek another form which will convey more completely the character of the color qualities and dimensions governing the range of pigments in regular use. Mr. Munsell has conceived this as a 'Color Tree' with a vertical trunk for the scale of Value and branches representing the different Hues, these branches varying in length with the Chroma Strength of each Hue.

* This is the Chroma of vermilion in dry form. Red printing inks are now made which are considerably stronger than ten steps of Chroma.

In the appended illustration the leaves of the Tree represent the measured steps of Chroma upon each branch.

"Upon the scale of Chroma the number of steps is limited only by the strength of pigments. The strongest yellow pig-

Fig. 8

ment in dry form, for example, will reach nine steps away from the neutral pole; but certain dyes on silk, or even printing inks and some unreliable pigments, may go one or more steps beyond this. As new and more powerful pigments may be discovered, they will add further steps to the scale of Chroma.

"We have described each of the three dimensions by which any color may be measured, and noted how each is written in a color formula. It remains only to put these separate notations together and to write a complete color formula embodying all three dimensions. For example, we are given a certain color to measure and define and we find that upon the scale of Hue it is purple-blue. Upon comparing it with the scale of Value we find it is but three steps away from the bottom, and that it is only two steps away from the neutral gray pole upon the scale of Chroma. A complete formula for this color would, therefore, be written P-B 3/2. It is scarcely necessary to point out the practical advantages of such a system of definite measurement and notation over the vague and variable terms in general use, borrowed from the vegetable and animal kingdoms, such as plum, olive, fawn, mouse, etc., of which no two persons ever have quite the same idea.

"It is hoped that the foregoing explanation of the three dimensions of color will have been sufficiently clear to convey to the reader a distinct mental image of what is meant by the terms, Hue, Value and Chroma, in order that we may proceed to the study of certain principles of order for the intelligent and harmonious use of color, which grow out of this simple and logical system of measurement.

Opposite or Complementary Colors

"The above diagram, displaying a circle of ten regular Hues arranged in the immutable order imposed by the spectrum, and reading clockwise, beginning with red at the top, will serve, with but little explanation, to illustrate what is meant by 'opposite,' or the possibly more familiar word 'complementary' colors. The term 'opposite' is used preferably in the Munsell System because it is simple and is self-explanatory, as will be seen by reference to the above diagram, where each Hue on the circle will be found directly opposite to another Hue. Thus a straight line drawn from red on the circle of Hues through the neutral pole will pass through blue-green, its opposite or complementary color. A line from blue through the neutral pole will pass through yellow-red and so on throughout the whole circle. It should be noted that each of the Principal

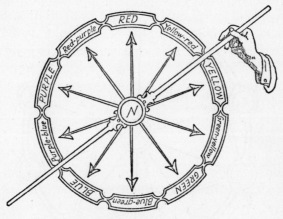

Fig. 9

Hues, red, purple, blue, green, and yellow, falls opposite an Intermediate Hue, blue-green, green-yellow, yellow-red, etc. Now two colors which are thus opposite to one another are not only farthest apart upon the diagram, but are in actual use the most strongly contrasting. It does not matter at what point we draw the line, whether it is from one of the regular Hues or from a point between two Hues, if it passes through the center it will fall upon the Hue or Intermediate Hue which is its strongest contrast. This may be more readily visualized if we imagine the spindle indicated on the diagram as pivoted on the neutral pole and movable to any point on the circle. The question may be asked as to how it is determined that these colors, which fall opposite to one another on the scale of Hue, are, in fact, the most strongly contrasting colors. The answer to this question will serve to demonstrate the logical foundation of the Munsell System. When any two colors are truly opposite or at the point of strongest contrast, their admixture * will

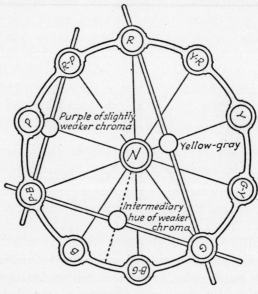

Fig. 10

produce a perfectly neutral gray. Though this may be accepted as axiomatic, it can easily be proved with scientific accuracy by arranging two opposite colors on a disk in proportions relative to the Chroma strength of each and revolving them with such rapidity that we cannot see them separately and they are mixed, when if they are truly opposite, they will unite in a perfect gray. Therefore working back from this fact, the scale of Hue has

* Using standard Munsell Maxwell disks.

been so composed that those colors which thus mixed with each other do actually make gray, are placed directly opposite on a line running through the neutral gray pole. Another question which may arise is what will take place if we draw a straight line between two Hues which are not opposites; and what would be the result of the admixture of these. This can be best answered by the accompanying diagram, where three different lines have been drawn, no one of them through the neutral center. These lines, it will at once be seen, cross points which are not neutral, but nearer to one or another of the Hues lying between the ones from which the lines are drawn, and the result of the admixture obtained is noted on the diagram. This will be sufficient to further demonstrate the simplicity and logic of the System and to suggest to the reader other interesting examples of it."

At this point in Mr. Cleland's essay on Munsell I shall omit further quotation and tell how you can make practical use of Hue, Value, and Chroma in painting in oils. Before you can master them, however, you will need to do a lot of experimenting—just plain mixing of this and that to see what you will get. I recommend that you try this frequently enough, even if you waste a lot of paint, so that you can be certain that you can mix exactly what you need. By this I mean that, if your eye tells you that you need a high-value green of weak Chroma for the sunny side of a distant tree, you can produce what you want with a minimum of messing around. Or, if you need a low-value, weak-chroma red for the shady side of an old barn, you will be able to proceed directly to the color needed. Only experience gained by experiment can teach you how to apply these principles.

Values and How to Get Them

Of all the attributes of color, most writers on painting agree that Values are the most important in a picture. At first I was a bit skeptical about this, but in time I became convinced. Perhaps the following suggestions will serve to convince you and make your progress more rapid.

All ordinary photographs are rendered in light and dark Values of one color, usually black or brown. Without question, the photographic picture is made with nothing but differing Values to depict shapes, design, form, and the like. Also all drawings made by pen and a single ink or by so-called "lead" pencils are limited to the use of Values to portray their subjects. In black-and-white photography, the trick of getting a good shot is largely a matter of proper lighting on the subject. This is merely another way of saying it is the Values that count most.

Wash drawings made with Lampblack on white paper are merely renditions of Values.

If you have ever tried color photography, where the general rule is to shoot the subject from the direction from which the light comes, you may have been disappointed because of the absence of something. That missing something is the virtual substitution of Hue for Value.

To understand the importance of Value, I urge you to do several paintings in a single color, such as Burnt Umber or Lampblack, using white paint to raise the Values when it is necessary. You will find that you can do a good picture with nothing more than a single color. But, if you attempt this, you will also discover that you cannot do a good picture by substituting Chroma (color strength) for Value or Hue for Value.

While it is vitally important to know that Value in color is more important than Chroma, this information is not a substitute for knowledge of how to get the right Value. Nor is it fair to say that any one leg of a three-legged stool is more important than the others. In my judgment, the place where an actual teacher of painting would be of the greatest help to a beginner would be in teaching him how to mix his paints to achieve the desired Values. Actual demonstration of such mixing, coupled with a running talk on the reasons why, would probably do the beginner more good than all I could tell him here.

Value lowering (far more difficult than Value raising) in a paint is achieved by mixing it with another paint of considerably lower Value. (In other words, we can darken one paint by mixing it with another darker paint.) Usually the best darker paint to use is a dark blue like Prussian Blue, Winsor Blue, or French Ultramarine. But there are other dark paints that are useful when occasion permits, such as Raw Umber, Burnt Umber, Payne's Gray, or black. Black, however, is generally disapproved by all writers and artists unless one mixes his own black from red, blue, and yellow. Such a mixture really does have a somewhat different effect in painting than the use of a black pigment such as Lampblack or Ivory Black.

The advantage of using a neutral Hue of low Value to darken another paint is that the Hue of the latter is not changed. Thus mixing a gray or black paint with some colored paint will lower its Value without changing its Hue. The disadvantage is that it not only *seems* to alter the Chroma, but, worse still, black mixed into a paint frequently produces a "dirty" effect that is difficult to define and, furthermore, may produce a "dead" color, also difficult to define. On the other hand, to lower a Value by the admixture of, say, Prussian Blue is to alter the Hue, thereby necessitating a further admixture of red and yellow to correct the excessive blueness. And this may introduce further complications: such an admixture is almost certain to change the Chroma in an undesirable manner, thereby requiring still further correction. For this reason I recommend starting with a paint that is as near to the desired Hue and Value as possible and altering it with the minimum admixture of other paints rather than starting out with the three primaries—red, yellow, blue—and mixing until the correct color is obtained. At the outset of your painting you should learn by practice how to work from the three primary colors, for only by so doing will you learn the trick of getting around in the three-dimensional maze of color. But, having acquired the knack by much practice, you should then adopt the short cuts, for they usually give a more pleasing result.

Color mixing is like threading one's way out of a maze. I have seen a young lady weep audibly over her inability to mix what she wanted. Nevertheless, it is almost as easy as falling off the proverbial log after one has acquired the skill. You should be prepared to waste gobs of paint merely to learn how to mix a desired Value, especially a Value lower than the Hue that results from your first mixing.

To increase or raise Values is fairly simple: merely add white. The converse should be equally simple, but the addition of black can give effects that clearly indicate that theory and practice don't always coincide. The addition of white, however, may introduce another problem—chalkiness. My way to avoid chalkiness is to start with pigments that are nearly right in Hue and Value in order to minimize the need for white paint.

CHROMAS AND HOW TO GET THEM

Up to now, I have not discovered any way of strengthening the Chroma of a paint, a process which would theoretically involve substracting some of the complementary, or opposite, color from the pigment. All that we can do to alter a Chroma is to lower (never raise) it by the addition of other different colors, the greatest reduction occurring when the added paint is the complementary color.

The best we can do is select those paints that naturally possess strong Chroma when we need a strong color and, when we need less color strength, either select a weak-chroma paint or weaken the Chroma of a high-chroma paint. But there is no known way of reversing the process. A pigment like Yellow Ochre is a low-chroma yellow of about 6 Value. Its Chroma, I should estimate, is about 5 or 6. This color property is something inherent in the mineral that is known as Yellow Ochre. There is no way of subtracting the complementary color, purple, from the pigment in order to achieve a higher-chroma yellow. If you want a higher-chroma yellow, you may start with another substance that possesses the property of absorbing more of the complementary color and reflecting more of the desired color. Such a substance might be Cadmium Sulphide, known as Cadmium Yellow. The difference between the Chromas of the two is marked, and I am not aware of any substances that are intermediate which are of sufficient permanence and chemical inertness for use as artist's colors. So, if we need a yellow of slightly stronger Chroma than Yellow Ochre's Chroma, we can add Cadmium Yellow, which has a stronger Chroma (about 12 to 14), to Yellow Ochre, or we can start with Cadmium Yellow and mix in some purple to reduce its Chroma to the desired figure. But there is no way of subtracting purple from the Yellow Ochre.

Take the flower of the wistaria as an example of a purple of strong Chroma that cannot be matched by any pigment known today. (Try painting wistaria some spring, and you'll find out.) The same can be said of the spiderwort blossom, which is a blue-purple. In the plumage of some birds there are colors that cannot be matched by any known pigment. A high-frequency electric discharge through a very high vacuum will produce a pale apple-green color of exceedingly high Value and Chroma that no artist could even approximate with any known pigments until Syan Green was discovered. There are many other examples of colors that we have seen but cannot match with existing pigments. Also there are many known colored substances whose color is so fugitive that most folks never even get a look at them. They might be available for paints were they more stable. Some of these substances possess color characteristics that cannot be matched by anything in nature.

FUNCTION OF HUE, VALUE, AND CHROMA IN ART

Now what good is all this discussion about color characteristics and about what the artists call "color theory"? How do we use it? My answer is fairly simple.

The proper *Hue* is used to give a realistic representation of objects in a picture.

The proper *Value* is used to give form to the objects. Shapes are depicted by shadows, or lights and darks.

The proper *Chroma* is used to depict by color the position or distance of an object from the observer. (This can also be done to a less satisfactory degree by the use of Value.)

These are basic rules, or principles, to be used in painting. Not blindly, of course, but as a guide for self-criticism. Often a beginner will reach an impasse with a picture. He will not know what is the matter yet will realize in a vague sort of way that there is something wrong. If an instructor or a competent critic can point out the error and tell him how it is to be corrected, the beginner will have a great advantage over one who is struggling alone.

But if you have to figure things out for yourself, it is very useful to know that the way to make objects appear to recede into the distance is to weaken their Chroma and that the way to weaken the Chroma is to mix in some of the complementary color, at the same time adding white to retain the Value. (Giving distant objects a bluish color often produces a similar effect.) It is also useful to know that the way to bring objects forward optically is to strengthen their Chroma. In fact, it is possible to make objects appear to protrude from the canvas by the use of very strong Chroma.

Such comments as, "Make that sky go *back*," may be helpful in telling you *what* is wrong. But if you need to know *how* to correct the difficulty, such comments are not satisfying. If your critic were to add that the way to make the sky go *back* is to lower its Chroma by mixing in a bit of the complementary color and then restoring the Value by adding some white, it would be far more helpful.

If one knows *what* to do as well as *why* and *how* to do it his progress toward good pictures is much more rapid.

In other places in this book I have stated that the technique of art is accentuation, or even exaggeration, of the characteristics of a motive, or subject, that arouses our own emotions so that the one who views our picture may be similarly stimulated. This accentuation can be applied to all aspects of a subject—not only to form, size, line, or Hue, but also to Value and Chroma.

Some people who know nothing about art are greatly impressed by the detail with which a subject is painted—something that is wholly unimportant. Many more, however, are impressed by the manner in which a flat surface (the canvas) can be made to look as if it had a third dimension, as if one could see far back into the distance behind the canvas. This is a mere device that is accomplished by the use of linear perspective and proper Chroma, the latter known to some writers on painting as "aerial perspective."

The term "aerial perspective" is used because the effect of

distance on colors is due to the absorption of part of the colors by moisture vapor and dust in the air. In the far distance the objects in a landscape have progressively lower Chroma, becoming grayer and grayer and finally acquiring a bluish aspect. This much is realistic. Some artists, however, exaggerate the changes of color caused by distance, displaying far more "color courage" than others. A. T. Hibbard and Chauncey Ryder are two such artists.

Another trick for making objects appear to be nearer or farther away is to use what are termed "warm" and "cool" colors. Cool colors are supposed to make things appear farther away. Although I can pass on to you the rule as I have heard it, I am unable to give you a definition of warm and cool colors that satisfies me. A warm color seems to be a color that is mostly yellow and/or red. A cool color seems to be one that is mostly blue. Alas, however, writers speak of Alizarin Crimson as a "cool" red, and also speak of "warm" green (which perforce must contain some blue). Where "warm" and "cool" find their line of demarcation I cannot guess. Art is still filled with inexact terms, like "rich" color which, so far as I can learn, has no artistic antithesis such as "poor" color or "lean" color.

This chapter on color theory has been a very condensed discussion of the vast field encompassed by that term. Its purpose has been to give you a nodding acquaintance with color. As you progress in your painting, you will want to study color theory further in other books or learn about it from different sources.

Plate II. SOLITUDE

me color sketches can be done swiftly. It all depends on the subject. This one (12 by 16)
quired less than an hour, compared to the more than one hundred hours needed for
e *Clam Digger*. The actual subject, near Saugatuck, Connecticut, has a multitude of
1all cottages just to the left of the house and is anything but lonely.

Plate III. PICTURES CAN BE PAINTED WITH FEW COLORS

This picture was done with four colors: Payne's Gray (which functioned as blue as well as for darkening other colors), Yellow Ocher, Burnt Sienna, and white. Richard Maritreu, the London portrait artist, whose clients include kings and queens and the world notables, suggested this simplification of the palette which, he avers, is ample for near all portraits and landscapes. It seems to place greater emphasis on Values, less on Hue and still less on Chromas. But the effect is pleasing without question.

FIVE

Paints and How to Use Them

BEFORE WE discuss the actual painting of a picture it is desirable to tell you something about the paints you will use and what you will do with them, what you will use them for. Here you will find the results of my twelve years of experience with various paints of the following types: whites, blacks, grays, reds, yellows, blues, greens, and browns.

WHITE PAINTS

White Lead is said to be a most satisfactory pigment from the physical aspect. It has a butter consistency that is supposed to be very satisfying. I have never used it because of the possibility of its darkening by conversion to lead sulfide from interaction with sulfur compounds in other pigments or from contamination in the air. That it can be used satisfactorily, however, is not to be denied, provided the painter uses proper care in "blocking it off," or isolating it, by means of varnishes or shellac from sulfur-bearing pigments. I do not recommend White Lead for a beginner because it presents too many problems; it is preferable to work with foolproof pigments rather than increase the hazards to a satisfactory picture. On the other hand, a beginner's first pictures are generally not worth saving except as mementos of an early struggle, so if White Lead is your choice for your first efforts no real harm is done. Furthermore, the discoloration caused by White Lead generally takes years to develop.

Zinc White is not liable to darkening from a slow chemical reaction with sulfur because zinc sulfide is also white. Zinc oxide, the white pigment, is a drying agent, and paint films in which it is used dry rapidly and become more brittle than those mixed with other white pigments. I have used Zinc White occasionally with fair satisfaction.

Perma Alba dries so rapidly that it forms a skin overnight when left on the palette. It is a satisfactory white for one who is doing a lot of work, especially for one who is painting every day and using it rapidly.

Titanium White is my personal preference because of its chemical inertness and its intense whiteness. Sometimes it is too white for easy handling—it dilutes other colors too easily—but this appears to depend on the fineness of its grinding. A fairly coarsely ground Titanium White is preferable to a very finely ground one because it avoids the excessive diluting effect that is difficult to control.

Titanium White is seldom sold in tubes in pure form. Usually it is mixed with zinc oxide; hence it partakes of a double drying character.

White is used more than any other paint. Buy it in 1-pound tubes provided there is room for this size in your box. Otherwise buy ½-pound tubes.

White paint is not always true white. You have only to compare several kinds of white on your palette to learn that some are whiter than others. Generally speaking, anything of a neutral Hue with a Munsell Value higher than 9.5 passes for white. For a beginner this degree of whiteness is usually satisfactory. It is only when you become an advanced student with several years of painting experience behind you that the whiteness of your white paint becomes important.

Regarding your use of white paint, the first rule of all is to keep it clean. This applies to colors as well, but because you dip into your white paint more frequently than into any other color, it is harder to keep it clean.

Two general effects are attained by the mixture of white with other paints. You lighten them—that is, you raise their Value— but at the same time you do something else that is not easy to describe. Robert Henri, in *The Art Spirit*, is one of the few writers who mentions this adverse effect of white paint—its diluting effect. I have observed it as an *opacifying* effect—a removal of the "depth," or semitransparency, a sort of dulling of brilliant colors when you want them strong but not too dark.

Sometimes you get a similar dulling effect by the use of too much painting medium, especially of one that contains a high proportion of turpentine.

Because of the diluting effect of white, I try to mix my colors from pigments that naturally have a high rather than a low Value. Thus a light neutral green will often have a more satisfying effect if it is mixed from Yellow Ochre than if it is mixed from a darker pigment like Raw Sienna and lightened by white. You will have to experiment a lot to learn how to control high Values. Sometimes, for instance, you will mix a dark, neutral greenish-brown, such as you use for wet rocks along the seashore, and find that it is a bit too dark; then, when a little white is added, the "depth" will go and it will be no good at all.

What is meant by "depth" in this sense I am unable to define accurately, but it is none the less real. For lack of a better explanation, I must say that apparently it is the same as semitransparency.

Probably my most important discovery, in the course of my self-teaching, has been that white paint can be used pure on canvas in small areas despite what many artists say to the contrary. I have heard professionals stoutly maintain that no one ever uses pure white, yet you need only visit galleries to see that this is not wholly true.

High lights often demand pure white. Look at anything about you and notice the high lights, especially if the objects are glossy and brilliantly illuminated. The arm of a red leather chair in my study is covered with the brightest red leather obtainable, but the high lights are white, not light red. Your eye fools you at times, though your brain tells you the light place is not white but red.

Art produces an illusion. Your skill as a painter depends upon your ability to produce the desired illusions.

BLACK PAINTS

It seems to me to be entirely appropriate to discuss black immediately after white, despite the fact that there are many intermediate Values between them. In the Munsell scale of Values, white has a rating of 10, which can be interpreted to mean that it reflects 100 per cent of the light falling upon it. Black, on the other hand, has a rating of 0, which can be interpreted to mean that it reflects 0 per cent of the light falling on it—or absorbs it all.

Representations of Munsell Values are, however, made with a matte surface. At the DuPont Finishes Dept. I have seen glossy-surface color card or swatches that rate Values of 00 and 000. These need not concern the artist, but they serve to justify the remark once made by a professional painter, "No matter how black you mix a color, someone else will come along with something blacker!" Yet, if 0 Value means complete absorption of all light, I am unable to explain 00 or 000 Values, for the equivalent of a vacuum in the field of light seems absolutely incomprehensible.

This brings up the question: What is black paint? Strictly speaking, I have never seen any. *Lampblack* is, in reality, a very dark, nearly neutral blue. While I have never seen Lampblack rated in the Munsell System, I should estimate it to be blue 1/1 or some such rating. You can easily discover that Lampblack is slightly blue by mixing it with white paint. In fact, such mixing with white is the only way for an artist to know what Hue is possessed by any very dark color on the palette. "Battleship-gray" paint is generally nothing but Lampblack in white paint. It is simple, permanent, and cheap—for house, factory, or battleship painting.

Ivory Black, on the other hand, is a brownish black, not a true black (however black it may appear on the palette), as may be demonstrated by mixing it with white.

The so-called "black" dyes of commerce are seldom true blacks. I once visited a silk-hosiery manufacturer at Northampton, Massachusetts, who told me they employed twenty-seven different "black" dyes, yet each one was different, and not one of them was true black. Incidentally, this seems to me to explain in part why old black clothing fades into greenish or dark yellowish Hues.

There are doubtless other kinds of artists' blacks than Lampblack and Ivory Black, but I have had no experience with them and know nothing about them.

A mixed black is usually more satisfactory for the artist than a paint made from a black pigment. The mixed black is made by mixing red, yellow, and blue paint until the result is exactly neutral, with no color predominating. To be sure that it is neutral, you have to remove a little and mix it with white, for only in that way will the true Hue be discernible. But don't put white into the whole mixture if you want to use it for darkening other paints.

When another color is mixed with black without any white added, the Hue and Chroma remain approximately constant, but the Value is greatly darkened. You can get some unusual effects by darkening certain colors in this way. For example, yellow (Cadmium or Hansa Yellow) gradually becomes a strong, dark green, like certain evergreens in late afternoon sunlight. You may think that this is the way to mix paint for evergreens (especially cedars), but if your experience duplicates my own, you will find that the Chroma or color intensity is far too great, and your tree will almost pop out of the picture instead of remaining in its proper plane.

Mixed with blues, black is sometimes satisfactory, but the mixture has a "dirty" appearance on the canvas. With red, such as Alizarin Crimson, black produces a strong, dark red that seems to be "clean" but often suggests a purple Hue.

My business experience in occasional bits of color printing has taught me a better way to use black than by mixing it with another pigment to secure an effect. For instance, to make certain blue letters possess proper clarity and depth, we used to order them printed in black ink first, then surprinted with blue, after the black had dried. Of course, we could have saved money by a single press run, using black and blue printers' inks mixed, but the result would not have been the same, nor would it have been as attractive to the critical eye.

Good effects can be obtained in the same manner in oil paintings when you are doing a serious picture, not merely a Sunday-afternoon sketch. Thus painting black on the canvas, letting it dry, and painting over it with a blue, suitably thinned, will give you dark blues that cannot be achieved in any other way.

I have read that a famous painter, whose name I cannot recall, painted a black cloak on a man by painting it first in a brilliant red and then, after the red had dried, painting it over in black. The red showed vaguely through the black and gave it a richness that was the envy of other artists for many years.

This matter of one color showing through another is a very
tricky thing, but by proper control it can be made to produce
effects that are otherwise impossible. I recall a large and pala-
tial sailing yacht that had a paint job that was the envy of other
yachtsmen. It was a sort of pale pink that no one was able to
duplicate. One chap fussed around with all manner of red and
white paints for more than two weeks trying to give to his craft
the glowing white of the big fellow. One day, in desperation, he
rowed out to the pink yacht when the owner was ashore and
with a knife scraped off a bit of the paint clear down to the
wooden hull. Then he discovered the secret. The big yacht had
been painted first with two coats of red lead and then with two
coats of white. The hint of red showing through the white was
what he had attempted—and failed—to duplicate by physical
admixture.

Optical blending is something that can be achieved in different ways. It is discussed in the chapter on mixing colors.

In my judgment there is more nonsense uttered about black
than about any other color. Most of it seems to come from
those who are only partially informed about painting. I have
had the experience of laying a palette with fresh colors in the
presence of ubiquitous spectators who immediately voiced their
objections to my use of black paint. At times I have been indul-
gent of such uninvited comment and, believing I could learn
something, I have asked the reasons for the gratuitous adverse
criticism. Invariably the replies have been inexact or unscien-
tific artistic jargon: "It has no life; it's dead." "You should never
use black." "My instructor won't permit me to use black or even
have it in my box."

Somewhere I read a story about an elderly dealer in artists'
materials in Paris who would never extend credit to a needy art
student if he once bought a tube of black paint. This old codger

believed that any student who used black would never sell a picture.

From my remarks you have probably concluded that black is a color that presents unusual problems. It does; decidedly so! Some artists get along famously without the use of any black paint at all. Others use it regularly. My experience is that one has a tendency to think he needs black more often than he actually needs it and that frequently some other color such as blue or brown is called for. Once I heard of a very competent teacher of water-color painting who always advised, "Whenever you go out sketching be sure to take your Payne's Gray along whether you ever take any other color or not." To be sure, Payne's Gray is not black (Munsell—o) but is about a 3-value neutral, supposedly made by mixing blue, red, and yellow, and as such does not meet with the howls that the professional objector-to-black puts forth.

In general, I think, black paint has a definite though limited use on the artist's palette. I should counsel the self-taught beginner to leave it alone for several years and then to use it only experimentally until he can control it. There will come a time when he will consciously want to develop form in his pictures by the use of greater contrasts between light and dark, and when that time comes he may find that black paint *may* (notice I said no more than *may*) be useful to him. But it must be used cautiously and sparingly until its use is mastered.

GRAY PAINTS

Nothing distinguishes a really good artist from his fellows so much as the manner in which he handles his grays. When, on going to an exhibition, I find that a well-executed gray produces an emotional response in me, invariably the artist turns out to have the well-known name of a truly great artist. I do not know whether or not other people respond to a well-handled gray in the same way that I do, but I do know that very few artists can do as well with gray as the masters, no matter how hard they try. The difficulty is that good grays are more a matter of the artist's skill than the happy choice of a pigment that is nearly right.

Arthur S. Allen, the colorist, once told me that when he has taught a class all it can absorb about color, his final examination consists of one test for all students: "Mix a 5-value gray." This, said Mr. Allen, is the most difficult task he knows in the field of color mixing. The fact that he thinks it the most difficult job of color mixing after a lifetime spent in the study of color (he was seventy-two years old when he told me this) probably explains why so few artists—even some professionals—ever become masters in the handling of grays.

The beginner is apt to want to purchase a tube of gray paint from the supply store. By all means, purchase a tube of Payne's Gray, and use it at times for darkening lighter colors. You will find other tubes, called "oil grays," available, but they are not intended for the artist's use in landscape painting. Their purchase is a waste of time and their use a waste of effort.

The most satisfactory gray is made by mixing Cobalt Blue with Yellow Ochre. A little white must be added before you perceive the grayness. This gray mixture possesses the much desired character known as "cleanness." French Ultramarine and Yellow Ochre also will produce a good gray when mixed in the proper proportions. It is odd that mixing a blue and a yellow produces a gray instead of a green, but the reason is that these two pigments are complementary colors.

Chroma does not enter into the mixing of grays, for grays are the very absence of Chroma. Despite the existence of the very useful Payne's Gray, the artist is on his own when it comes to painting in the neutral colors that border on true gray or true neutrality. For, no matter what color you start with, the addition of its complementary color will result in a gradual neutralization of the initial color until it finally becomes gray (true neutrality) of whatever Value it may be, while further admixture of the complementary color will tend to make the mixture partake of the color being added.

What, then, shall we do with *Payne's Gray?* Plenty. But first let us consider the constitution of Payne's Gray. According to books on artists' materials, this color is made by mixing red, yellow, and blue until true neutrality is attained. Nothing is said about *what* red, *what* blue, or *what* yellow, and the paint manufacturer never gives any data on the label of his tubes. Furthermore, I have seen some so-called Payne's Grays that I have strongly suspected of containing much Lampblack. This may account for the "dirtiness" sometimes produced by mixing a color with this gray when it is in the high-value range. At any rate, Payne's Gray has been on the blue side of neutrality in every tube I have ever purchased. This, to me, suggests the possible presence of more than a trace of Lampblack, but perhaps Payne's Gray is mixed that way.

Payne's Gray is not black. Its Value on the neutral scale is about 2 or 3. I have found it useful for darkening colors rather than for graying them. This, however, is not really a necessary use, for often darkening can be obtained by leaving out white, which is a far better method of obtaining low-value colors than putting in black or Payne's Gray.

You will probably learn by your own experiments that, if you put too much white into a color mixture and attempt to darken it by the addition of black or Payne's Gray, you will arrive at a color different from the one you thought you were going to get. The converse, where you have darkened a mixture and want to make it lighter with white, will be almost as unsatisfactory unless you have mixed your own black from red, yellow, and blue. For color is a three-dimensional phenomenon—Hue, Value, and Chroma—and unless you understand thoroughly what you are doing with it you will generally arrive somewhere else than the place you thought you were going. All too often you may think you are moving up or down the Value scale and will find you have been moving sideways on the Chroma scale, or vice versa. But still more often you will find that you have been moving along a three-dimensional diagonal by three simultaneous changes.

One easily acquires bad habits in painting, just as in other human activities. Hence I advise beginners never to try to neutralize a color by mixing it with gray, whether it be Payne's Gray or any other. The only correct way to gray a color is to mix it with its complementary color and keep on trying until you get what you want.

When I speak of grays in landscape painting, I include the colors that are nearly gray along with true neutrality. These will be all the Hues having Chromas up to about 2, of whatever Values you may elect to employ from 0 to 10 (black to white). In theory, a little of one color mixed with a lot of a neutral color of the appropriate Value should give a satisfactory neutralization of the color employed. But theory and practice have the sad habit of diverging at unexpected times, often for good and sufficient reasons. In this case, however, the reasons have never been clear to me. The commonest explanation for dissatisfaction with this method of neutralization is that it produces a "dirty" color.

Payne's Gray has a use that I recently learned from Richard Marintreu, the London portrait painter. He suggested that I try painting with only four colors: Payne's Gray, Yellow Ochre, Burnt Sienna and white. The Payne's Gray and white would serve as a neutral blue. Since my return from London I have had very little time in which to paint, but I have managed to do one sketch with these four colors. It is very different from anything

I have ever done before (see Plate III), and I like it well enough
so that I want to do several more when time permits. The
Payne's Gray and white make a very satisfactory sky, though
one more delicate than anything I am accustomed to doing.
And the same gray also serves to give the greens, functioning
here as a blue.

I repeat that the way an artist handles his grays is a dead
giveaway of his ability. And I know of no more difficult color
problem in painting than matching the gray of old weather-
beaten boards as they appear to the eye at the approximate
distance from the artist for a landscape painting. Really to
master the use of the neutrals requires a lot of experimentation
and experience as well as the know-how and know-why.

RED PAINTS

In landscape painting, red seems to be more difficult to use
than green, yellow, or blue, probably because we see red so
seldom in the landscape. It is only for a few days of spring and
a few weeks of autumn that red is with us, and those times are
too short for us to be as thoroughly acquainted with their reds
as we are with the greens of summer, the browns and near-
whites of winter. Consequently, we are not as well prepared,
visually speaking, to paint reds as we are to paint other colors.

Only an artist of considerable experience can comprehend
and analyze the play of colors in a scene that he sees only a
few weeks in a year. It takes prolonged study and observation
to discover what these colors really are. And, alas, mature experience will show you that they are seldom what they appear
to be. But first let us discuss red pigments.

Alizarin Crimson is the old stand-by for the reds. It is not,
however, a pure primary color. It has a bit of blue in it, which is

the reason artists often refer to it as a "cool" red. If it had yellow in it instead of blue, they would probably refer to it as a "warm" red. Alizarin Crimson is a transparent color rather than an opaque one. It has a medium Chroma, at least the kind that comes in tubes does. And it dries slowly. You seldom need to throw it away because it has dried out even if you can paint only once a week. It has no special peculiarities that I have been able to note. It is what I should term a "must" for your palette.

Harrison Red, also an organic color, is a good permanent red that is naturally lighter and contains more yellow than Alizarin Crimson. I use it occasionally, but I do not regard it as a particularly important red for beginners. Though it has proved convenient to me for painting red flowers in the landscape, its yellow factor makes it impossible to use in mixing all the purples I sometimes want. If you were completely deprived of it, you would suffer no serious inconvenience.

Rose Madder is a transparent red, the beauty of which is apt to attract the beginner, but except for flower painting it has a limited utility. This is because of its weakness, or weak Chroma, and its transparent character. On account of its weak Chroma you may find it easier to manage when you are beginning to paint, but, after you have worked at painting long enough to acquire confidence and skill, you will probably prefer Alizarin Crimson, which has much more power. I have carried a tube of Rose Madder in my box for years and have scarcely ever used it.

Chinese Red and *Chinese Vermilion*, like Rose Madder, have little use for the landscape painter. As colors I admire them, but every time I squeeze them out on my palette I wonder what I am going to do with them.

Cadmium Red is, however, in a very different category. Here is a very useful scarlet-red of strong Chroma and considerable application. You will always want this color in your kit. It comes in Light, Medium, and Dark, and my experience shows that Light is preferable, for it is fairly easy to darken a light Hue, but it is next to impossible to lighten a darkened color by the admixture of white without altering its character in a manner that is undesirable. In other words, the darker Cadmium Reds are less manageable than the Light.

Up to now I have never been able to mix yellow of any description with red of any sort and produce a Hue that is the equivalent of Light Cadmium Red. Perhaps it can be done, but I suggest that you benefit by my waste of paint in this futile attempt and not try to duplicate it.

I have found Light Cadmium Red particularly useful for painting certain types of red buildings, particularly when they are in the sunlight. There is no substitute for it that I have been able to discover. Yet, though to me it is indispensable, I find that I seldom need more than a mere speck of it on the average picture.

Burnt Sienna is a reddish-brown paint, of mineral origin, that is more nearly red than any other Hue. It is treated here as one of the reds, for it is useful in painting autumn foliage and certain foregrounds—like dry grass in an August scene when there has been little rain. This useful color should be on your palette for nearly every picture.

Artists'-supply stores have other reds in stock that may lure you into their purchase, but you will have little use for them.

Again, I want to repeat that red foliage in the autumn landscape is probably the most difficult to manage of all the Hues you will encounter. Well do I recall a professional artist who visited Roxbury, New York, in 1939 or 1940, in a particularly vivid autumn. Local inhabitants say that after two days of effort in which he had not produced a satisfactory sketch, he began to jump up and down in a rage, screaming, "How do you paint autumn colors? How?" This substantiates my statement to the effect that we see autumn colors so few times in our lives that we have greater trouble with them than with almost any other subject—unless, perchance, it be blue skies. These we see nearly every day, but they are always a difficult problem for a very different reason.

Part of the problem of autumn reds arises from the fact that they are not often actually red. A truly red tree is a rarity. More often they are neutral oranges, of both high and low Value—some redder and some yellower. (Burnt Sienna with Light Cadmium Orange often give a fair approximation of autumn colors.) And as autumn closes some foliage, like that of the oak, which holds its leaves until late winter, becomes a light brown. Memory often plays mean tricks on us, and this is especially true of our recollection of autumn colors a half year later.

Yellow Paints

In my attempts at self-teaching, I have found more difficulty in the handling of yellow than any other color—except red. Reds come first in my own order of difficulty and blues last. As I have tried to analyze my troubles with yellow, I have come to the conclusion that they are caused by the availability of a greater range of yellow pigments than of the other Hues. By "range" I mean the actual pigments, not merely the Hues. These pigments in the Munsell System of color identification run in Chroma from 0 to 14 or 15. No pigments of comparable range of color saturation have been discovered in other Hues, so far as my knowledge goes. There are, of course, many fugitive pigments of strong Chroma that are useless for any but a very brief time—certainly useless for the artist. Some of these are known to fade in a few months, which suggests that they are unstable chemical compounds.

There are several good handbooks on the chemistry of yellow pigments, but they will tell you little about their use or about their optical characteristics. Those that I have read imply that Cadmium Yellow is the strongest yellow (has the strongest Chroma) available. But I have found that the International Printing Ink Corporation has a yellow printing ink known as *Hansa Yellow* that is considerably more intense than Light Cadmium Yellow. It is so much cheaper than Cadmium Yellow that I have used it for years—at least ten—and have yet to discover the least sign of fading or other undesirable chemical properties. A quarter-pound of Hansa Yellow will serve me for all my week-end painting for two to four years. On account of its strong Chroma much less of this color need be used than is true of other yellows of weaker Chroma.

Another reason why I like this particular Hansa Yellow for painting in oils is the fact that it is more nearly a pure primary color than any other yellow I know. Although I am not exactly parsimonious, I do dislike waste; and one of the easiest ways to waste paint is to mix colors in a fruitless effort to arrive at exactly what you want. Such waste can frequently be avoided when nearly pure primaries are available. Hansa Yellow contains almost no red—so little, in fact, that when it is mixed with a nearly pure blue, like Winsor Blue, it is possible to get a close approximation of Emerald Green. Not that there is much need for Emerald Green; I mention this merely to show the absence of red in Hansa Yellow.

Some artists have laughed about my use of printer's ink for an oil color. Well, what is printer's ink, and what is an artist's paint? The difference is very slight. For practical purposes, the ink is a pigment ground in varnish while the paint is a pigment ground in linseed oil. And since the artist uses both oils and varnishes I see no reason for quibbling.

For a beginner Hansa Yellow has no special merit over Cadmium Yellow, because initial attempts at painting are seldom worth saving. When you have advanced in experience, however, I believe you may be justified in acquiring Hansa Yellow for a trial. But I must warn you that I once purchased a tube of Hansa Yellow from an artists'-supply store when I was assured that it was the identical pigment ground in oil instead of varnish (and hence more plastic, or soft, and more easily used) and found it to be miles away from the real thing so far as Value and Chroma were concerned. It is said there are several Hansa Yellows, which may account for my disappointment. And my admiration for Hansa Yellow should not be taken as any disparagement of those who choose to paint with the better known pigments.

Cadmium Yellow is available in Light, Medium, and Dark. If you use any of these, I think you will find that Light Cadmium Yellow will serve all your needs. The other two have limited uses and apparently have more red in them. Dark Cadmium Yellow differs but little from certain Cadmium Oranges.

Extra-pale Cadmium Yellow does, however, have its uses, and I recommend either it or *Zinc Yellow* for your palette. The Extra-pale is useful for certain light greens that cannot be matched with Light Cadmium Yellow. On the other hand, Zinc Yellow is weak in Chroma, and there is nothing you can do about it if you need a stronger yellow.

The Cadmium Yellows and Hansa Yellow dry very slowly and remain usable on your palette for many days, whereas Zinc Yellow will dry rapidly enough to form a skin overnight. In fact, any paint that has zinc in it will dry rapidly, zinc being an accelerator of the drying of linseed oil. Zinc Yellow has few uses and can easily be omitted from your painting kit without impairing your freedom of action unless, perchance, you need rapidly drying paints. But rapid drying can be achieved easily with driers or by the admixture of earth pigments.

Talens Yellow possesses a yellow quality that differs from anything I have been able to mix from Hansa or the Cadmium Yellows. I have found it very useful in painting yellow autumn foliage, and I recommend it for your autumn painting. At other times you will have little use for it.

Yellow Ochre is next on your list of important yellows. It is a mineral pigment (an "earth color," in artist's lingo) of weak Chroma (about 5 or 6) in contrast to Cadmium Yellow (around 12) or Hansa Yellow (15 or 16). In other words, as a neutral light yellow of about 4 or 5 Value, Yellow Ochre is a paint for which you will find much use. To be sure, you can neutralize Cadmium or Hansa Yellow with purple until you approximate the color of Yellow Ochre, but why waste the time and the material? Yellow Ochre is very cheap. Besides, even if you were to neutralize a strong yellow to match Yellow Ochre, it would have a different drying rate—much slower— and it might not always meet your needs.

There are also other Ochres, such as *Golden Ochre*, which, though I have used them considerably, have no special characteristics to recommend them.

Mars Yellow is a neutral orange-yellow that I have used occasionally; there is also *Mars Orange*. But aside from their use in autumn colors they have been of little value to me. Some professional artists find both very useful, but I am not sold on them yet.

Raw Sienna is another mineral pigment that I include in the yellows, though some might call it a light brown. It has a very weak Chroma and low Value, dries rapidly, and is a color everyone should have on his palette.

Gamboge, for the sake of the record, is a liquid, colored, gumlike, transparent material which has more uses in water-color painting than in oils. Because of its transparency, it is occasionally useful for glazing over dark-green foliage to simulate the effect of golden sunset light falling on trees. Because of its extremely limited use, you will probably not miss it if you never have a tube.

Aureolin is another yellow of limited use. Its Chroma is very weak. In water color it is useful to depict sunlight on green grass, but not so in oils. I recommend it for water colors, but not for your oil kit.

If my suggestions are followed, you will have on your normal palette: Extra Pale Cadmium Yellow, Light Cadmium Yellow or Hansa Yellow, Cadmium Orange, Talens Yellow, Yellow Ochre, and Raw Sienna. Talens Yellow can be omitted in most cases without inconvenience.

To become proficient in painting, as in all other activities, it is important to have experience. All that I can write or all that any teacher can tell you will not be a substitute for actual experience in mixing and applying colors to canvas. Yet there are some suggestions that may save you precious time when you are trying to catch a fleeting impression or make the most of a few hours away from your regular vocation.

Sunlight on green foliage, especially when it shines through the leaves, is often better represented by a very light yellow of strong Chroma than by a light green. Direct sunlight changes everything from its normal color under a blue or gray sky. But this use of light yellow can be overdone; it should not be followed as a mechanical rule, for sometimes the high light is really a light green. The only rule is to experiment until you hit on what you want.

The yellows of autumn foliage have, to me, always been dif-

ficult to match. In general, I have found that Yellow Ochre
and white or Raw Sienna and white make fairly close approxi-
mations of autumn yellows. Here is where Talens Yellow has
also often been helpful.

Light, high-value, and strong-chroma Yellow is usually the
high light of green foliage. Light, high-value and weak-chroma
Yellow is usually the high light of yellow. It's curious how our
untrained eyes deceive us and how we learn after years of painting that things are not often what they appear to be. Snow is
seldom white. Red trees are almost never red. Black is usually
dark blue. And many a so-called "blue" sky is pale green.
Clouds are not white, and red sunsets are never so red as we
think they are.

Art is the creation of an illusion, the final test of which is the
finished picture and its effect on others—besides your admiring
or hypercritical family. The mixture on your palette may seem
just right but on the canvas may be no good at all, while some
colors on the canvas of a great picture, if seen alone on your own
palette, might tempt you to scrape off and start afresh.

No color can be properly judged until it is on the canvas
adjacent to other colors and until the effect of them on each
other, indoors, has been considered.

BLUE PAINTS

When I first started painting in oils someone persuaded me
that Prussian Blue was sufficient for each and every purpose.
Probably you know the type: "All you need is Prussian Blue,
Alizarin Crimson, and Cadmium Yellow." (Few people seem
to know that there are several different Cadmium Yellows that
are not exactly interchangeable.) Such partial information,
given without regard to its limitations, is not helpful to the
untutored artist. Experience has shown me that there is no

one-purpose blue. You will need several blues if you are going
to strive for perfection in the rendering of your ideas.

Of course, there is one blue that has fewer limitations than
the others, but I have never found it successful for all purposes,
even though it comes closer to being a pure primary color than
any of the other blues. This is one of the new synthetic colors
sold under several trade names. I have found that Winsor &
Newton's *Winsor Blue* is the most satisfactory of the several
makes that are stated by supply dealers to come in this class
of oil colors.

Winsor Blue is an excellent blue to have on your palette.
It may fool you, for, as squeezed from the tube, it has a purple
cast which at times resembles French Ultramarine. But as soon
as it is mixed with other colors or white the difference is quickly
evident.

While I have never seen a Munsell Color analysis of Winsor
Blue, my guess is that there is a wee hint of yellow in it. Hence
it possesses a faint suspicion of green, which is not objectionable in many skies but makes it difficult to use to produce certain blue-purples—such as the shadows on snow under a very
blue sky. If you are one who is easily satisfied, you will find
this blue the most nearly satisfactory all-purpose blue of all.

Prussian Blue has a much stronger Chroma than Winsor
Blue—at least 16, perhaps even higher, compared to Winsor
Blue's Chroma of 10 to 12 or less. Because of Prussian Blue's
strong Chroma, with its very low Value, it is difficult to manage;
a little of it overpowers all other colors in a most disconcerting,
if not discouraging, manner. It is, moreover, far from being a
true primary blue, having a decided greenish Hue which becomes all too apparent when you want to mix a strong blue-
purple; the amount of yellow in it neutralizes the purple to a
disappointing extent.

Pictures that "reek" of Prussian Blue are the earmark of a

beginner who has not been adequately warned of its hazards. Back in the middle 1930's, when there were many exhibits of WPA art projects in large cities, the telltale Prussian Blue was the most characteristic feature of the pictures produced—except, of course, their subject matter. The latter was generally on the theme of social protest.

We all must go through the beginner stage, but when we emerge from it we have generally left Prussian-blue themes far behind us. Nevertheless, I would not condemn this color wholesale, for it has its uses, and invariably I have it on my own palette in small amounts, just in case I may want it in a hurry.

But Prussian Blue has the faculty of staining bristle brushes, seemingly dissolving in the fibers, and a brush so stained must be thoroughly cleaned, or it will introduce a hint of blue into other colors when blue is not wanted. To avoid this staining, use a red-sable brush, though sable may not always give you the sort of brushwork you wish to employ.

If you must mix Prussian Blue with other colors, you will find it a wise procedure first to mix a little of it with white to increase its Value to proportions more easily controlled and then to work from this. Or else mix white with Prussian Blue until you reach the desired Value (lightness or darkness of blue), and then add your other colors until you get the exact Hue, Value, and Chroma desired. Otherwise you are apt to clutter up your palette with huge quantities of paint, most of which will be of little use to you, while attempting to mix the small amount that you are going to use.

French Ultramarine deviates from a pure primary blue on the purple side as much as or more than Prussian Blue deviates on the green side. It is, however, a far more pleasing color to me than Prussian Blue. I find it necessary on my palette and would not be without it. But I find it is impossible to mix certain chartreuse greens—pale, high-value, strong-chroma yellow-greens, like the sun shining through grass in early spring—from French Ultramarine because of the neutralizing effect of the small amount of red in this pigment.

In days gone by I have observed certain purple shadows in snow pictures in galleries where professional work of a high order was on exhibit and have then gone home with the high resolve that I, too, should be able to mix similar colors. I have wasted quantities of paint in a futile effort to get what I imagined I was after, only to learn in time that the particular Hue was obtained from mixing French Ultramarine and white. I mention this experience because I have found that some colors cannot be obtained by mixing—and the reason is that there still are no pigments available to us that are pure primaries of strong Chroma.

Cobalt Blue is another valuable pigment which seems to have color properties that cannot be attained by any mixture of other paints. It is much lighter in Value and a trifle more purple than French Ultramarine. Its utility is not so great as the latter's, and hence, though you should always have it available, you may find it unnecessary to put it on your palette for every picture.

An excellent clear gray can be made by mixing Cobalt Blue with Yellow Ochre in proper proportions.

Cerulean Blue, a pale neutral blue (ladies might call it a "pastel" blue) looks a lot better than it is. Apparently its name, meaning "sky blue," makes the unwary believe that it is the open-sesame to proper sky colors, which are the despair of the artist for the first few years of his training. If my own experience is any criterion, a tube of it will last you for your entire life. On days when I am filled with ambition, I frequently put it on my palette and then scrape it off, unused, after it has become hard and dry, wondering what on earth possessed me to put it on in the first place.

While we are on the subject of blues for blue skies, I want
to tell you of two other colors that are very useful for sky painting but are not really blues at all; they are greens. One of these
is Cobalt Green; the other, Syan Green.

Remember that blue skies are not always blue. Sometimes
they are a high-value, neutral blue-green. Such a pigment is
Cobalt Green, which I discovered after five years of painting
and used for a while, later abandoning it. Cobalt Green is far
more blue than green, and while it can be approximated in Hue
by mixing other colors it is handy for autumn sunsets or late
afternoons when the sky, seen above the flaming foliage of
October, appears quite green—light, but nevertheless green.
When you are working rapidly to capture a fleeting impression,
it is disheartening to have to mix and mix for some time when
the color that is nearly right can be squeezed from a tube.

I am going to introduce you to a color at this point that few
artists know about and many will doubtless chortle at its mention: *Syan Green.* This is available, so far as I know, only in
the form of printer's ink from the International Printing Ink
Corporation. Syan Green is a synthetic organic color, like
Alizarin Crimson and Hansa Yellow, and is permanent as well
as chemically inert with respect to the various substances used
by artists. It is an exceptionally blue blue-green of exceedingly
strong Chroma and, as near as my eye can tell me, is totally
devoid of red. It reminds me of the green of the traffic light.
And, though I believe anyone would consider it a green, if you
mix it with Alizarin Crimson you get—not brown—but purple!
It is also a transparent color and tremendously powerful. My
guess is that it has a Chroma stronger than Prussian Blue, ap-
proximating the Chroma of Hansa Yellow—which means, of
course, that a very little of it goes a long way.

A quarter-pound tube will undoubtedly last the ordinary

Week-end Painter his entire lifetime. It is not essential to your equipment, but if you are a perfectionist you will find that certain sky colors that defy you can be mixed with Syan Green as a starter.

You are not to take this discourse on Cobalt Green or Syan Green as gospel or as the considered opinion of a master of the art of oil painting. I am merely sharing with you some of the discoveries that I have made during my experiments in teaching myself how to paint. You will have to experiment on your own account, even as I have done. Because my education was originally that of a research scientist, my experiments in this complex field of art may possibly be a trifle more systematic than those of a person without similar training, and they are given to you for whatever use you can make of them.

All painting is an experiment. You try this and you try that to achieve an effect that is in your mind or imagination. An artist who does not experiment with new methods, new ideas, new techniques is not much of an artist. If all that an artist (or anybody else) knows is derived solely from what is taught him, he is limited to the knowledge of his teacher. Great artists, those whose names are famous, have all been great experimenters, both in techniques and subject matter.

This does not mean, alas, that all experimenters in art are great artists. In art, as in most other activities of man, most experiments turn out to be of little value and must be discarded. Were it otherwise, we should all be rich, be great artists, musicians, scientists, manufacturers, etc. But without constant experiment we cannot improve. This is my justification for trying out colors like Syan Green and Hansa Yellow.

GREEN PAINTS

Green is the Hue we think we see most in our lives. This is especially true of the artist who paints out of doors, for generally his efforts outside are in the warm weather when greens predominate.

But the right green for foliage painting is a color you never purchase in tubes. Most of your green paint you will make for yourself by mixing blue and yellow. There are, nevertheless, other reasons for having in your kit certain of the manufactured greens, such as Emeraud, Permanent Green, and Green Earth.

Emeraud is not identical with Emerald Green, which books on painting condemn, but looks something like it. It is a medium-chroma blue-green that is sometimes useful for the greenish blue of autumn skies. It's worth having in your kit, though you will have about as infrequent use for it as for Light Cadmium Red.

Permanent Green is a medium-chroma yellow-green or green-yellow-green. I seldom find any use for it, except to have it handy on the palette to use for neutralizing a red. It merely saves time and material to have a green all ready instead of stopping to mix a green when your palette may be pretty full of other colors anyway. It comes in both Dark and Light, the latter being preferable.

Green Earth is a mineral pigment, having a neutral-green Hue. I purchased my only tube of it because I had read somewhere that Corot used it as a starting point for the smoky green foliage of his later period—the period when his pictures achieved their greatest popularity, though critics do not regard them as his greatest works. If you never own a tube of Green Earth, you will not be seriously handicapped.

In my discussion of blues, I mentioned Syan Green and

Cobalt Green which are so much more blue than green that I shall not mention them further here.

The commonest use of green is, of course, for painting foliage. The commonest error of the beginner is to make his foliage too green, that is, to give it too strong a Chroma. The beginner usually forgets, or does not know, that the green of foliage has a weak Chroma. It has a lot of red in it. I do not recall ever seeing a picture of a green tree, for example, where the green was overneutralized. Corot made his trees almost neutral gray. But I have seen plenty of landscapes where the foliage was painted a poisonous green that fairly cried out for neutralization with red.

Here is something that may serve to fix the point in your consciousness. If some green leaves are macerated in a suitable organic solvent that will dissolve the chlorophyll (the green coloring matter of foliage), the solution will be green by reflected light. But, if you place it in a transparent glass container and hold it up to daylight, you will discover that by transmitted light the solution is deep red—not green. There is really a tremendous amount of red in chlorophyll. When mixing greens for landscapes, don't be afraid to add plenty of red.

The foregoing does not necessarily apply to painted green buildings, although if the paint on them is old and weatherbeaten it will require some neutralizing, however green it may have been when new.

Strong greens are often needed for painting still life, textiles, and figures, but I shall not discuss these subjects here.

Brown Paints

Brown can be mixed from blue, red, and yellow in the proper proportions, but there are two manufactured oil paints in the

brown category which you should have on your palette for the
sake of convenience—if for no other reason. These are the
Umbers—Raw Umber and Burnt Umber. Both are of mineral
origin (earth colors), dry very rapidly, and have Hues that are
fairly close to each other. They differ chiefly in their Chroma;
Raw Umber has a Chroma of about 2 or 3, while Burnt Umber
is about twice or three times as great. As pure tube colors, both
are very dark and not easily distinguished except after mixing
with white.

Up to now I have never seen any essential difference between the Umbers of different manufacturers. One make seems
to be as good as another, which is also true of the Siennas. But
this does not apply to all colors, for there are some paints
where the best is none too good.

The Umbers are useful as starting points for many of the
browner aspects of nature.

Speaking of browns, many people confuse dark yellow with
brown. Furthermore, it is very difficult to say where brown
leaves off and neutral red-purple begins. Lady painters are
wont to exclaim enthusiastically about "purple-browns" in the
background of a winter landscape.

Brown comes in the class of what some writers call the
"secondary" colors, because they can be produced by mixing
red with green, which is itself produced by mixing blue and
yellow. While this may be useful as a method of instructing
little children, it is not, in my judgment, strictly true. For there
are indeed few colors that an artist puts on a canvas that are
not really admixtures of the three primary Hues.

But I shall not press the point here. If you find that it is
helpful to you to consider all colors as separated into primaries,
secondaries, tertiaries, and so on, far be it from me to oppose
this concept. The colors remain what they are, regardless of

what some artists, colorists, and critics may say or think about them.

Both Raw Umber and Burnt Umber exhibit a very strange property when mixed with a strong yellow like Cadmium Yellow. The resultant color is not brown but a strong olive green!

SIX

Mixing Colors

EVERYONE IS entitled to his own opinions as to the propriety of any procedure in painting, yet I consider it an unmitigated evil to make a statement to the unsuspecting beginner as if it were a proved fact when, in truth, it is merely a matter of opinion. Such a statement was once made to me ex cathedra in my early days of painting by an artist of many years of experience. He rated as a professional artist and was giving me a criticism that had been solicited. And I accepted the dictum from my better without even suspecting that he was merely stating his own opinion—an opinion that several years later I discovered to be of almost no value for me. Here is what he said: "I don't want to see any raw color on your canvas. Mix your colors *well*, on your palette, before you begin to paint."

Therefore I proceeded to mix my colors thoroughly for at least four years, thereby acquiring what I now regard to be a bad painting habit—one which since then I have found it almost impossible to control. For nowadays I want to avoid this too thorough mixing in order to produce something of the "vibrancy" of colors utilized by the French Impressionists, which is based on the optical blending of colors rather than on the physical mixing of pigments. Yet, because of the habit of thorough mixing which I gained by a noncritical application of this artist's advice, as soon as I get deeply interested in a picture I can seldom remember not to mix too much.

Therefore I give it to you as my *opinion* that the mixing of colors can be overdone, also that there are two general procedures to be employed in mixing color on the palette: complete mixing and partial mixing. My advice to the self-taught artist would be to consider each carefully and consciously to utilize whichever technique will produce the desired results. Bad habits in painting are as difficult to overcome as a bad slice in golf or smoking too much. Another bad habit, that will be discussed separately in the appropriate chapter, is brushing too much, but this is generally acquired long before one ever picks up an artist's brush and is even more difficult to overcome than overmixing.

To understand why I consider overmixing bad it is necessary to learn more about what artists who have graduated from art schools would call "color theory." The name is far more formidable than it should be. So please read Chap. IV, "How to Find Your Way in Color," before you read further in this chapter.

In my own experience in painting I have found that sound theoretical knowledge permits me to proceed more quickly to the solution of a color-mixing problem than would be the case were I always forced to proceed by the time-consuming process of trial and error.

CHOICE OF COLORS

So many books have been written on the components of colors—as, red and blue make purple, blue and yellow make green—that I see no point in repeating in this book, which is written for the purposes of the self-taught artist, what has been said elsewhere over and over again. You are urged to study many books, for what I am attempting to say here consists principally of things I have had to learn that have not been included in any of the art books I have read.

Suppose you are going to mix a green for the tree foliage in a landscape. We will further assume that this is for a small canvas

about 12 by 16 inches, because the problems of painting trees
that are very small are somewhat different from those of painting trees that are large (see Chap. XV "How to Paint a Tree,"
for details). Take some blue with your palette knife, and place
it on a clean space on the palette. Then wipe off the blue from
the knife, and take some white. Then mix this with the blue
until you obtain the Value (lightness of the blue mixture) that
approximates the particular part of the particular tree that you
intend to paint on your canvas. You may need to add more
white or more blue to get the approximate Value needed. I
should add that this is a very crude approximation, for the
successive additions of yellow and red will lower the Value of
the mixture. Hence there is no point in extreme accuracy at
this point. The mixing should be as little as possible if you follow my plan of operation. There will be streaks of blue and
white in the mixture.

I have not told you what particular blue to use, for that all
depends on whether you need a strong green or a neutralized
green. Whenever you need a strong-chroma color you must
start with a strong-chroma primary, because whatever is added
to a color results in a degradation, or lowering, of its Chroma
(color strength). There is no possible way to increase the
Chroma of a single primary color by the admixture of some
other color. This is the resultant conclusion that everyone
much reach after experimentation. And it is due to the fact
that there are very few known substances that possess the ability
to reflect a high percentage of any wave length of the white
light that may fall on them.

The optical, or physical, phenomenon that we call "color"
deserves explanation at this point. Color, such as we know it, is
a psychological phenomenon. Among those who should know
best, there is a belief that there is no such thing as color in
nature; it's all in the eye and brain of the beholder. What are

Plate IV. THE CLAM DIGGER

Well over one hundred hours of actual painting went into this picture, in contrast to the short time spent in doing Solitude. The *Clam Digger* was based on a black-and-white newspaper reproduction of a photograph by Adolph Fassbender.

called "colored" substances are materials that absorb certain wave lengths of light and reflect others. The reflected ones that reach our eyes have varying effects on the complex chemistry of vision and produce the mental impressions we know as colors. As I attempt to translate physical science into art and to interpret art in terms of physical science I reach the following generalization: Some substances have the property of absorbing more light energy than others; consequently their reflection is less. If the light that is reflected consists of a small band and comprises a very few angstrom units, we have what is popularly known as a "primary" color. It possesses a single Hue that cannot be analyzed by the prism into any subsidiary or component colors. To this extent it corresponds to the older concept of the atom of the chemist or to a single letter of the alphabet.

As far as I am aware, there are no known substances of opaque characteristics that reflect light rays within the extremely narrow zones of wave lengths that I postulate as being *pure* primary colors. Alizarin Crimson, though predominantly red, possesses a little blue, Prussian Blue possesses a little yellow, French Ultramarine possesses a little red, and Cadmium Yellow possesses a little red, in addition to their predominant wave lengths. Therefore, strictly speaking, there is no such thing as a true primary pigment, but there are a few pigments that are close enough for practical purposes to be used as such in painting. Hansa Yellow and Winsor Blue come pretty close to perfection in this respect.

Pigments have another characteristic that must be reckoned with, for not only do they vary with respect to the wave lengths of light that they absorb or reflect, but also they vary with respect to the amount of total light that they reflect within the specified wave lengths. Some reflect a high percentage, while others reflect a low percentage. Those which reflect a high percentage of a single, narrow wave-length band are the strong-chroma color pigments. Those which reflect a low percentage of the incident light within the given narrow wave band but also reflect other colors are the weak-chroma color pigments. Where the proportion of the total incident light reflected is high, we have pigments of high Value, and, where it is small, we have pigments of low Value, that is, darker colors.

All of this refers to the colors of opaque substances—pigments—and does not refer to the matter of colored light.

If you are not thoroughly familiar with that device known to all artists as the "color wheel" or "color circle," you will find one in Fig. 11. You should know it so well that you can draw your own from memory at any time without reference to a textbook. The color circle refers to what are described as "primary" colors. From the beginner's viewpoint, the primaries are red, yellow, and blue. Nevertheless, there are some authorities who say there are five primaries: red, yellow, green, blue, purple. Others say there are six primaries: crimson, red, yellow, green, blue, violet. One writer insists that there are thirteen primaries. And then we also have the names of the colors of the spectrum: red, orange, yellow, green, blue, indigo, violet.

Names, names, names! Merely words. The array of colors is still the same, some preferring one group of words, others preferring another.

The most important thing for you to learn in constructing your color circle is that the Hues on opposite sides of the circle are complementary colors.

If you are as serious as I hope you are, you will find that this excursion into scientific principles has an important bearing on your understanding of the techniques of painting. For you really must learn to know the limitations of your materials. After you have mastered these limitations, you will begin to appreciate the consummate skill of the great masters of painting and to admire what they have done.

To me, the limitations of the pigments that artists use can
be roughly compared to the limitations of the musical qualities
and ranges of notes of the various instruments of a symphony

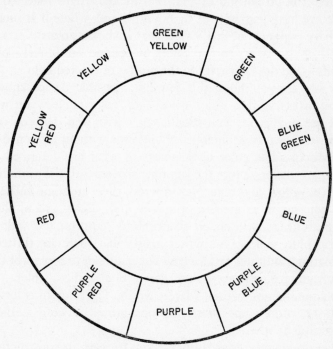

Fig. 11. The Color Wheel

Each of the colors is shown in sequence around a circle and opposite
its complementary color. Every artist should be able to draw a color
wheel from memory. Until you can do this you should always have a
copy in your kit. Opposite colors are important to know when you
want to gray or neutralize a color without changing its Hue.

orchestra. There are string, wind, and percussion instruments
that have a composite range from the lowest note of the contra
octra bassoon to the highest note of the violin and piccolo.
While my acquaintance with symphonic composers is not

large, I have never heard or read of one bewailing the fact that he could not order a stinging high note on the double bass nor sorrowing over the fact that the flute could not give out a window-shaking diapason.

As an artist-to-be you are probably unconscious of the fact that you are about to tackle a job comparable to the job of the composer for the full symphony orchestra. (You will notice that I do not limit this to a small orchestra.) Besides, unlike the composer who must depend on the big orchestra to portray his creations, you will have every material thing available for your work that the greatest artist ever had. In this respect you will also have as many materials with which to work in the sense that the unabridged dictionary is available to every author.

If you firmly comprehend the fact that no pigment except a theoretically pure white (which does not exist) can reflect all the light that falls upon it, that any colored substance reflects only a part of the light that falls upon it and absorbs the rest, you are ready for the next step. As soon as you add a second color to the first, the mixture of the two (when well mixed) will absorb still more of the incident light and reflect less, albeit of a different Hue. So, if you add some yellow to the blue that we left on your palette several pages back, you will get a green, but it will seem to be slightly darker than either the blue or the white mixture or the yellow which you added to it. (An artist friend of mine disagrees with me on this last point.) If you started with a strong blue and a strong yellow you will have a strong green—a strong-chroma green—though its Value will be slightly lowered.

Now you are ready for the third step—that of neutralizing the green, because the greens of foliage have so much red in them. You should begin to add a very little Alizarin Crimson to the green in successive amounts until the proper graying, or neutralizing, has been accomplished. While you are doing this, you will observe that the green becomes darker as well as more neutral. This phenomenon used to bother me a lot until I realized that by adding another pigment I was absorbing still more of the incident light, which meant, of course, that the resultant color was darker, or that its Value had been lowered. The only way to bring back the Value, or lightness, is to add more white.

Now before we go on to other aspects of color mixing, I want to explain something else. All the immediately preceding discussion has been based on the mixing—the thorough mixing—of pigments. They have been mixed as though they were to be used as house paint, and no unmixed, or "raw," color, to which the artist objected at the beginning of this chapter, is visible.

Suppose, however, that we utilize optical blending instead of physical blending. You will realize, of course, that this is a sort of a figure of speech. For it is, to my way of thinking, a physical impossibility to employ 100 per cent optical blending, at least in the sense in which I propose to try it.

First of all, you must realize that our eyes play all manner of tricks on us, and I like to utilize one of these tricks. If light-blue dots are intermingled uniformly with light-yellow dots and they are placed close together, when viewed from a suitable distance the dotted area will be light green. If light-blue lines are intermingled with light-yellow lines the surface will also be a light green. (The use of colored dots or lines is the very basis of process, or three-color, printing, as can be observed by inspecting a colored reproduction under a magnifying glass.) There will be a difference, however, between the green produced by the juxtaposed lines, dots, or gobs of blue and yellow, and the same amount of the same pigments mixed with the same amount of white and reduced to a uniform blend. The difference will lie in what is popularly known as "vibrancy" of color. As I have rationalized this to myself, juxtaposed colors do not suffer the same lowering of Value that occurs when these same colors are physically mixed; yet the color impression they produce on the eye is near to that which is the result of actual mixing, only with both a higher Value and a stronger Chroma, or color intensity. As some folks put it, partially mixed colors have a vibrancy, or "life," that make them more attractive in effect than thoroughly mixed pigments.

Since I have always been rather fond of the paintings of the great French Impressionists and have tried to appropriate some of their techniques, you will readily see why I am not an advocate of the thorough mixing of color on the palette. This, however, is merely my own peculiar opinion of the proper way to mix color, and I do not attempt to impose my ideas on others. And I daresay you will find many accomplished artists who will scoff at the foregoing ideas and may attempt to persuade you to do otherwise. Which is as it should be, for art is not standardized, and there are an infinite number of ways of interpreting your own ideas in paint on a canvas.

Another method of mixing color that is advocated by some writers and condemned by others is to mix it on the canvas itself. I regard this as an expedient to be utilized only when it seems to be well-nigh impossible to mix the correct Hue, Value, and Chroma on the palette because there are other adjacent colors on the canvas that modify the impression in a way that cannot be foreseen.

Summing up the methods of mixing: we have complete mixing; partial mixing, which is the more difficult to control; and the secondary method of mixing a small amount of color on the canvas itself.

Which colors to mix is a matter of personal choice and is governed only by the limitations of the pigments. Except where you definitely know that you are going to want a neutral color it is better to start with the strong-chroma colors and work toward the grayness you desire, for to work toward a higher Chroma theoretically involves *unmixing*, which is impossible and wastes a lot of paint. The best help I can give you here is to urge you toward a lot of experimentation. Only by long experience will you get to know your colors and how to manage them. All that anyone else can do for you is to suggest reasons for your expecting this or that result from a given procedure.

What quantity of color to mix so as to cover a given area is also a matter to be determined by your own experience. Much depends on the size of the area and on whether you paint thin or heavy—whether you thin out your color with a medium or whether you "lather" it on in a sort of impasto or bas-relief, modeling in color, as it were. It is a good plan, however, to mix too much paint rather than too little, for beginners find it almost impossible to match a color that has been reached after considerable trial.

Excess mixed color need not always be thrown away if your palette has room to hold it. Sometimes you will find that such leftover color can be used elsewhere. But such economy often carries with it a very definite hazard, for it may lead to the formation of another bad painting habit—the injudicious utilization of bits of unused paint. This habit can lead to the production of drab pictures that lack the zest and sparkle of pictures painted with fresh colors that have not been over-neutralized. To comprehend the difference, please imagine yourself listening to two persons talking, one of whom has an enunciation that is thick, fuzzy, and monotonous, while the other sparkles with vigor, clarity, and a well-modulated voice. There is little doubt as to which one you would prefer to hear.

I know of one Week-end Painter who nearly always finishes his pictures with all the paint left on his palette, apparently

imbued with the erroneous notion that it is a sin to throw away
a color, regardless of how it may detract from his completed
sketch.

And I know of another self-taught artist who has acquired
the habit of mixing Dark Cadmium Red with many of his
colors for some reason that is, of course, his own prerogative;
yet he frequently complains of the muddy character of his
paintings. It is my humble opinion that he would do much
better if he would eliminate this pigment from his palette. Its
use is extremely limited.

Good, clean painting that has the much admired quality of
"freshness" does not require a prodigal waste of colors, but it
does need self-control and, perhaps, a resolute scraping off the
palette of all mixed colors that have no real use. If you have
some paint left over it does not necessarily belong on your
canvas or mixed with something else. Throw it away before you
waste good color trying to work it in where it does not belong.

Clean, fresh painting is most frequently produced by starting with colors made of pigments that are close in Hue, Value,
and Chroma to those you desire. Mix as few other colors into
these as possible, and apply with a clean brush so as to avoid
the further inadvertent admixture of still other colors.

There is another matter to consider in your choice of colors
for mixing. The average Week-end Painter wants his picture
to dry rapidly. This seems to be characteristic of most beginners,
although an experienced artist, who may want to work on a
picture for several days in succession, occasionally wishes it to
dry out slowly. There are times when the mature painter wants
to work on a dry canvas and others when he wants to work
on a wet one. Your choice of the pigments with which you paint
can exercise a very considerable degree of control over the
rate of drying. You have only to look at the paints on your

palette to discover, a day or two after you have used them, which ones remain wet and which dry rapidly.

In general, the earth colors dry very quickly, and any mixture in which they are present will dry almost as quickly. These are the Siennas, the Umbers, Yellow Ochre, Naples Yellow, Green Earth, and Indian Red. Also included among the rapid driers are Cobalt Blue and Prussian Blue.

Among the slower driers are Hansa Yellow, all the Cadmium colors, Alizarin Crimson, Winsor Blue, and French Ultramarine. The strong yellows all seem to be notoriously slow driers.

A color mixture made entirely from slow driers will be a slow drying mixture, while one that includes even a very little of a rapid drying color will usually be a rapid drying mixture. All this may not be very important, but it will serve to explain some of the differences you may encounter.

~~~~~~

SEVEN

Limitations of Pigments

IF YOU have ever worked with a focusing camera and have viewed the inverted image on the ground glass under the focusing cloth, you have probably been greatly impressed by the gorgeous colors visible there and nowhere else. Alas, no artist can ever reproduce those colors with the pigments available today. For the colors that have been concentrated by the lens and projected onto the ground glass are not pigments but colored light of high intensity. Until self-luminous pigments have been discovered, the artist must work with materials that reflect from o to a maximum of about 60 foot-candles, whereas the actual light intensities in nature range from o (total blackness) to about 1,000 (light as bright as the eye can bear). These measurements have been made by a Weston or General Electric light meter for photographers.

Landscape painting will always be a method of creating an illusion, not an approximation, of nature. The colors we *see* in nature are transparent, while those with which we paint are principally opaque pigments. Even at their best, nonluminous pigments cannot reflect very much light, yet with such paints the artist produces a picture that, if skillfully done, *seems* to have as much light in it as nature itself, *seems* to have the emotionally stimulating colors of nature. I say *seems* to have as much light, because the light meter will quickly convince you that it does not.

One day when doing a landscape I used my light meter to measure the light reflected from the principal objects around me. Here are the results. (See also Fig. 12.)

78

Foot-candles

Sky	85
Tree foliage	25
Sunlight, foreground	25
Shadow under trees	4
Tree trunks in shadow	1

Fig. 12. Light-meter Readings on a Subject

The artist must render the divergence of light intensities occurring in nature by light reflected from his paints on the Munsell Scale of Values of from 0 to 10. Careful light-meter readings in foot-candles on this subject, on a day that was not particularly bright, showed that the sky was 85, the foreground in the sun and the sunny side of the willows was 25, the shade under the trees was 4, while the shadowy side of the trunk of a tree was only 1.

Thus it will be seen that there was a maximum difference in light Values of the order of 85 to 1, which had to be rendered in pigments differing from the lightest to the darkest in the

order of about 10 to 1, as expressed on the Munsell Value
Scale.

There is nothing mechanical or mathematical about art. No
rigid formula can be followed. But such measurements as these
may help you to realize a little better how you must make the
utmost use of the limited "reflectability" of your paints in order to create the desired illusion in your pictures. In the absence
of an instructor, perhaps the light meter will help you in self-
criticism. The biggest single step upward that I can recall
having made took place when, by such an analysis, I realized
how I had been limiting myself in this matter of Values.

EIGHT

Painting Mediums, Thinners, and Driers

SOME WRITERS of books on painting mention painting mediums, and some omit all reference to them. Still other writers
give quick discourses on various mediums but omit instruction
as to their use: how to use them, when to use them, and when
not to use them. So what I have to say in this chapter is derived
solely from my own experiments and observations.

WHAT IS A MEDIUM?

A medium, in oil painting, is merely some form of thinner to
make the paint more fluid or less plastic. Anyone who ever
painted a floor knows how much easier it is to brush out a thin
paint than a thick one. (I must emphasize with all the force at
my command, however, that brushing experience gained from
painting a floor or a wall is a total loss when applied to the painting of pictures. In fact, it is the source of one of the worst habits
an artist can acquire. Another bad habit is the indiscriminate
use of thinners.)

Some professional artists say they have never heard of painting mediums. One of them was once looking over my equipment with considerable amusement, because I usually carry
the equivalent of a small artists'-supply store around with me.

"What's that?" he asked, pointing to a can smaller than my
turpentine can.

"That's my painting medium."

"And what, pray, is a painting medium?"

"Mine is a mixture of oil of copal, stand oil, and linseed oil."

81

"I never heard of anything like it before. Where on earth did you get on to it? Or is it one of your own inventions?"

The strange thing to me is that this chap is not alone in his apparent unfamiliarity with the use of painting mediums. I occasionally go out sketching with an artist, the quality of whose work I would give my eyeteeth to duplicate. One day he came over to where I was working to borrow some matches and paused a moment, finally exclaiming, "What in blazes is that stuff you are using in that cup?"

"Painting medium."

"Never heard of it! What good is it?"

Incidents like these came early enough in my painting career to cause me to be very questioning in my experiments and to paint pictures both with and without the use of painting mediums. From this experience I give you my conclusions as to their merits.

BENEFITS FROM USE OF MEDIUMS

When a medium is mixed with tube paint in moderate amounts, the paint becomes very soft—even fluid if too much is used. The painting, however, goes very rapidly, far more rapidly than it would if you were to use the thicker paint as it is squeezed out of the tubes. This speed is important when your time is limited, for the hobby painter never has as much time as he needs. He may be able to paint on a Saturday afternoon and a Sunday, and then, if he has not completed his picture, he must await another week end. And another week end may be rainy, the scene may be wholly changed, or business or family cares may interfere.

With the aid of a medium, the first stage of painting a picture may be completed in a very short time, leaving the remaining painting hours for the really good work. I will admit that I also get an odd sort of satisfaction from the way the brush slips along when the paint is thinned by a medium.

Less Desirable Effects of Painting Mediums

While the negative aspects of mediums do not outweigh the desirable ones, it is well to know what they are so that when you run into them you will not be disappointed in the results.

First of all, too much medium can make colors so fluid that they will run. Remember that easel painting is done on a surface that is approximately vertical, and very wet or fluid paint will run down and perhaps ruin an area that is fairly good. If you are painting in your home, you can expect to find drops of thin paint on the rugs or floor which, if discovered by the lady who is married to you, may lead to some uncomplimentary language. Thick paint seldom falls to the floor.

Second, the use of a medium that contains much turpentine does something to the paint itself which is not easy to explain. You can observe this most easily by trying it out with pure turpentine. The wet paint turns lighter and becomes chalky in appearance. For underpainting—that is, the first stage of covering your canvas with paint—this color change is not objectionable, provided the paint film is not so diluted that a picture holds on to the canvas by sheer faith alone. It is to avoid a mechanical failure of the paint film that I use the mixture of thick stand oil and oil of copal (not picture copal), seldom thinned with turpentine, for my medium.

Sometimes I add the slow-drying raw linseed oil if I have time enough to work on a picture for several days—as when I am on a vacation and want the picture to dry very slowly. At other times I have added various varnishes, mainly to see what would happen, and have as yet discovered nothing, despite predictions that Damar varnish, for instance, will turn yellow with age. (Maybe I'm just plain lucky.) And I have also added a drier to my medium, frequently at the close of a two-week vacation when I have had a dozen or two freshly painted canvases to transport.

Third, a medium leaves considerable gloss, or shine, on the surface of a painting. Often the picture will appear to have been varnished.

Fourth—and here I am indulging in pure speculation—you might paint a really good picture with a very thin medium, like a 36- by 48-inch canvas I once saw in a rented home. The picture was a part of the furnishings. It was fairly dirty, and because the subject was interesting the tenants decided to clean it with soap and water. The dirt came off, all right, but so did an area of the picture about the size of a man's hand, exposing the bare canvas. They wanted me to try to paint back the missing area, but I ducked that assignment.

I have a hunch that pictures as fragile as that one was are painted with the aid of a very thin painting medium and that if the artist had used more paint and less of the insubstantial diluent he would have achieved greater permanence.

The best advice I can give is to avoid too much turpentine in your medium and to make it up of fairly heavy polymerized oils like stand oil. Turpentine is to be avoided, for it evaporates, leaving little residue. Also it alters the appearance of the paint, making it appear chalky.

You can paint just as good a picture without a medium, but it will not progress so rapidly.

Unexpected Results

I was once out painting with two other hobby painters, two of us working in oil and one in pastels. The pastel worker was by far the best artist and produced an exquisite landscape. But it appeared to have been done in oils. One of the oil painters produced a very good picture of the same subject that looked as if it had been done in pastels, for it had that opaque, chalklike appearance that we associate with pastels. This artist had used too much turpentine in his painting. The other, myself, produced an oil painting that resembled a water color more than it did an oil, largely, I believe, because I had used too much of a thick, heavy medium. No one of us had painted with his colors just as they came.

It was an occasion of great merriment and provided ample excuse for a couple of rounds of the kind of beverages that cheer after a cold day outside, followed by a hot dinner and an evening of discussion of the relative merits of our efforts and all the techniques of art. A day like this with good companions, all intensely interested in the same subject, is one of the greatest escapes I know from the harassing problems of business.

ABOUT DRIERS

If you are going to use a drying agent with your paints, such as Japan Dryer, you should put it into the medium. Some writers condemn the use of artificial driers in art work, but I have never seen or heard a good reason for not using them. While I have not made a profound study of the uses of artificial driers, I am unable to believe there is anything evil about driers as a *class* of catalytic substances that should cause them to be banned altogether. There are probably some good driers and some bad ones. I am inclined to believe that the wholesale condemnation of driers is really a condemnation of their *overuse*.

A journeyman house painter once told me that most inexperienced householders who try to do their own decorating are apt to use ten to twenty times as much dryer as they should.

"It just kills the paint," he added. But, when I tried to find out in what way the paint was "killed," I could get nothing that was truly informative.

Ordinary observation will reveal to anyone, whether scientifically trained or not, that there is very little substance in a drier and that what there is can hardly be considered a substitute for the oil in a paint film. Hence, if an excessive amount of drier is added to a house paint, it requires no profound imagination to realize that the paint film will be diluted by a liquid that possesses very little nonvolatile substance. Conceivably, the molecules of the oils will be so separated from each other by dilution that when they dry they will have very little cohesion. And, if this hypothesis is correct, you can then expect to find a very weak paint film that will probably be chalky—meaning that it will rub off because it lacks binding power or cohesion. If a paint film "fails" because of the addition of a drier, therefore, the failure must probably be blamed on mechanical causes rather than on interference with the complex chemistry of the oxidation of a drying oil (though, of course, there is also a possibility that too much drier leads to too much oxidation of the drying oils.)

I believe my hypothesis is a valid one, because exactly the same sort of phenomena can be observed by the addition of too much turpentine, and I have yet to find an artist or house painter who will condemn the use of moderate amounts of turpentine. So it seems to me that a *small* amount of drier may be used in an artist's paints without doing any harm. If the acceleration of drying by chemical means were harmful, then certainly we should condemn the use of all the earth colors (Ochre, the Siennas, or Umbers), for if there ever was a substance that will catalyse the oxidation of drying oils it is this class of very useful pigments.

Furthermore, I have been using DuPont's Japan Dryer for

the past eight years without yet observing any harmful effects. To be sure, the real test of time is not eight years, but centuries. Nevertheless, I doubt if any hobby painters are painting for posterity in the year 2500. Posterity can better be served by those professionals who have the opportunity to spend their entire lives at the work we love but can pursue only as an avocation.

What I have said about driers has been a sort of parenthetical explanation in the discussion of the use of mediums in paint. There is, however, another digression that logically belongs here—one on the use of "anti-driers," or slow-drying oils.

SLOWING DOWN THE DRYING RATE

There are times when you will want your picture to dry very slowly rather than very rapidly. This is accomplished by the use of painting mediums containing no drier but to which has been added an oil that will dry very slowly. Raw linseed oil will do this, but some books call for poppy-seed oil. I have had a bottle of it at home for years but have never had occasion to use it. It is my opinion that the need for extreme slow drying comes at a stage of progress far beyond that of the average Week-end Painter who works only for pleasure.

The reasons for wanting fast- or slow-drying pictures are found in one's desires to paint on a wet or dry surface. The effects are vastly different, and, as your experience grows, you will quickly learn which you prefer. As a rule, you will find it better to paint wet paint on wet paint, piling it up, rather than to put wet paint on dry paint. There are exceptions, of course.

Before leaving the mediums it might be well to recall that some famous painters used mediums and diluents. Paul Cézanne is reported by Ambroise Vollard to have painted with colors thinned out with turpentine to such an extent that the wet paint dried almost "instantly," to quote Vollard's own words. Cézanne's pictures are probably not yet old enough to reveal whether this dilution of the paint film presents a serious problem for their owners. At any rate, I have never heard any reports that they are crumbling or dusting away.

NINE

Brushwork

PAINT IS applied to the canvas with a brush or a palette knife, although other implements, including the finger, are sometimes used. There was once a story current around New York that a group of artists on Cape Cod were using putty knives for painting, but I have never been inspired to try this.

Brushwork has frequently been given an aura of mystery by art critics who, perhaps, know more about the emotional appeal of art than about the craftsmanship that must go into it. And it is with that craftsmanship that we are most concerned in this book.

I have been able to gain less information about brushwork from other persons than about any other aspect of the craft of painting in oils. This may be because many artists are either secretive about their methods of applying colors or are annoyed by anyone who watches them closely.

Once I chanced to see an artist in a curious performance. His movements reminded me at times of a fencer; at others he seemed to be doing some sort of an aesthetic dance before his easel, with one arm extended behind him while the other held a ½-inch brush in a long-radius, graceful upward swoop, his whole body springing up from the ground where he apparently started from a squatting position.

Curiosity got the better of my good judgment. By dint of cross-examination I was able to learn that by this movement he had drawn in a single curving reed that leaned forward from a shadow into the sunlight. Its line was as graceful as the reed itself and was only about 1⁄16 inch wide, yet had been executed with a ½-inch brush! It was a revelation to me to make this one observation, for it not only told me why he did not want to be watched, it also revealed untold and unsuspected possibilities in the techniques of handling the brush.

A famous French painter is said to have folded up his kit and gone home in a rage if anyone—even the owner, an old lady out tending her goats on her own farm—paused near him or came within eye range of his work.

Most of what you will be able to learn about using the brush will be derived from your own experiments supplemented by reading or from taking instruction under a teacher.

ARTIST'S BRUSHWORK IS NOT HOUSE PAINTING

I cannot repeat too often that the worst experience for the beginner is experience in painting floors, woodwork, and furniture, for all such commendable activities around the home develop exactly the opposite of the proper technique of handling the artist's brush. In house painting the object is to brush out the paint into a thin film of uniform thickness, whereas the artist should use the brush to put the paint exactly where he wants it and *then leave it alone!* If house-painting brushwork is carried over into picture painting, you are almost certain to have muddy colors and little brilliance in your pictures. The only place where brushing out is a good technique is in laying on large areas of paint on a *fresh* canvas—for example, in rendering a clear sky in which the colors must blend gradually and smoothly from the darker blues at the top to the lighter Hues at the horizon.

If you discover that you are brushing *a là* house painter and cannot break yourself of this bad habit, the best thing to do is paint with the palette knife, for with this tool you can lay on the color but will find it much more difficult to mess it around and ruin its cleanness and freshness. Nevertheless, even with the palette knife it is possible to smear and dirty a canvas.

Put the paint on with the brush or palette knife, and *leave it alone!* (See Fig. 14, between pages 92 and 93.) If the color is not to your liking, then either lay another color on top of it, or scrape it off and replace it with the other color. If you lay one color over another wet color, however, and begin to brush it, at that point your painting will begin to go backwards. If the last color you applied is the proper one for that particular spot, brushing will mix it with the improper color that is underneath, and the more you brush the worse will be the mess. There is no remedy but self-control—one of the most difficult of all things to acquire.

Sizes of Brushes to Use

All writers seem agreed on one point: Use the largest possible brush that does not make your line too wide. This principle, however, must not be accepted blindly, for the consistency of your paint will make a difference. When you are generous with your medium, the brush mark will be much wider than when the paint is thick. Also the length of the bristles will make a difference; old and worn bristles, being shorter and stiffer, do not splay out as much as new brushes. Then, too, brushes come in two lengths of bristles, those with longer bristles being called "Brites." While I make no recommendation to others as to bristle length, for my own painting I prefer the shorter ones.

A brush will make a wider line than its apparent width would indicate. Van Gogh's bold brushwork appears to have been done with very wide brushes, but when I copied one of his paintings I learned differently. I found that a ¼-inch brush produced a ⅜-inch mark when I used the amount of medium which seemed to be necessary to duplicate Van Gogh's style.

Another rule of thumb regarding brush sizes: Use a big brush on big pictures and a small brush on small pictures.

Still better advice comes from the author of a book on painting who notes that, because objects appear smaller in the background than in the foreground, large brushes should be used for foreground painting and small ones for objects far away. But this rule should not be followed blindly. There are times when a narrow brush is most desirable, as for doing a sort of mosaic of color, in the Cézanne manner, in a foreground.

ROUND VERSUS FLAT BRUSHES

Both bristle and sable brushes come in flat or round shapes. Most painting is done with a flat brush, but there will be times when you will find a round brush more suitable, as for the painting of the branches of trees. I have also found that applying paint with a sort of rolling motion of the brush goes much better with a round brush than with a flat one. This type of brushwork is sometimes used for painting foliage. It produces irregular patches of color.

Small round brushes are satisfactory for producing very narrow lines, as for showing the rigging of a ship, but a good artist seems to be able to make any sort of line with almost any sort of brush.

BRISTLE VERSUS SABLE BRUSHES

The beginner will have little need for Russian-sable brushes, which are very expensive. Even the advanced student will use them only occasionally. Yet there are times when only a sable will serve a need.

Sable hairs, being very soft and pliable, leave no marks as bristles do. When you wish to paint very smoothly, the sable

Fig. 13. EASY WAY TO HOLD A PALETTE

A lazy man's way of holding a 16-by-20 palette and a towel is to put them onto a water-color easel. This leaves the hands free for better purposes. On the oil painter's easel is a partly finished painting of the same subject shown in Fig. 15, the picture on bath-towel technique.

Fig. 14. PALETTE-KNIFE TECHNIQUE

One easy way to avoid dirty color or to lay wet paint over wet paint is to paint with a palette knife. The paint is transferred to the canvas on the tip of the knife. Foliage and leaves on the ground are knifework. The idea is to put the paint on and leave it alone. Don't muss it!

Fig. 15. BATH-TOWEL TECHNIQUE

The soft grass in the foreground was painted by laying in the correct colors with horizontal strokes of a bristle brush. Then the grass was dry-brushed vertically with a small roll of bath towel, working successively from the top toward the bottom to avoid cutting off the tips of the grass. A clear place on the towel must be used for each stroke, or the paint will smear.

Fig. 16. TOOTHBRUSH TECHNIQUE

Foreground and foliage in an autumn gale were first painted in the normal manner, then dry-brushed with a bent toothbrush to produce a type of softness intermediate between normal brushwork and the bath-towel technique. The toothbrush must be wiped *clean* between strokes.

Fig. 17. EFFECT OF SCRAPING OFF A PICTURE

An unexpected result was attained when an unsatisfactory picture was scraped off by vertical downward strokes of the palette knife with the intention of salvaging the canvas panel. The resulting misty landscape pleased so many persons that it was left as it is here

Fig. 18. THE COMMONPLACE IS IMPROVED BY ELIMINATION

I passed this scene thousands of times on my way to and from work. One day it appealed to me as a suitable subject for a picture. My first effort, however, was most unsatisfactory until I painted out a lot of horizontal branches projecting from the pines. Simplification and elimination help materially.

Fig. 19. PAINTING A TREE

1. Draw the bare tree. Then cover the lines with a thin wash of cobalt blue in turpentine. Dotted lines show general limits of the masses of foliage. Paint in the sky between the masses.

2. Paint the trunk and principal branches with suitable dark colors. (The faked buildings in this sketch were merely incidental and later were changed.)

3. Following the plan of painting from back to front, the back foliage is painted next, also some of the parts of the buildings.

4. Parts of the foliage on the near side are painted, especially the higher Values at the sides of the tree. The nearest parts come later.

5. Continue painting the higher Values in the foliage masses, increasing the Chroma of the greens for the nearest foliage.

6. The completed sketch. The unsatisfactory buildings were relegated to the background in an imaginary valley by the simple expedient of painting over them.

Fig. 20. A SKYLESS LANDSCAPE

By selecting and eliminating you can make a large number of different pictures from the same subject. This was done from the subject that also inspired Plate V (the twelve element picture). Instead of painting in the sky, the canvas was left bare. The muggy July day and drooping foliage suggested the need for vertical brush strokes.

Fig. 21. REFLECTIONS IN WATER

In muddy water or in clear water over a dark bottom reflections are grayer than the object reflected. At midday they are nearly as light in Value as the original. When the sun is low, the reflection has only about half the light-meter reading of the object reflected; hence it is darker as well as grayer.

is useful. It is also useful when laying wet paint over wet paint where you need to avoid picking up any of the lower layer of paint and thereby making the colors muddy. But the sable should never be used for rough work like scrubbing in a color, or for so-called "scumbling," which, I believe, is but another way of saying the same thing. All this does is wear out a very expensive brush on a job where a bristle brush would serve better.

Brush Marks

Brush marks in the paint are all a part of the picture you are painting. These tiny ridges cast small shadows and indicate the direction in which the brush has been drawn. A succession of such marks gives movement or direction to the eye as it contemplates the picture. The coarseness or fineness of the brush marks does much to suggest the character of the subject depicted. A smooth, flat surface, such as a wall, would not be as well represented by paint laid on with coarse brush marks as by the smoother texture of paint that had been laid on with a palette knife.

Problems of "Softness"

The painting of grass, especially long grass, or of waving grain or of rushes in a swamp gave me no end of trouble for many years. Everything I painted in this category seemed to be stiff and sharp. Sometimes grass that should have been silky and long looked as jagged as broken glass! It seemed to me that I would cut my shoes to pieces if I could walk into my own pictures. And then I would study again the works of the great landscape painters in the Metropolitan Museum of Art in New York, the National Art Gallery in Washington, and the

Art Institute in Chicago, wondering how on earth those other fellows did their work. The technique of Renoir in particular got a lot of my attention.

One day I dropped into a dealer's gallery in Chicago to see a Corot he had on sale. I learned that the dealer had known Corot many, many years ago, and that led to a discussion of the brushwork Corot used in painting his trees, which are often so like wisps of vapor. There is one Corot in the Metropolitan Museum in New York, I told him, that has a distinct fingerprint near the edge of the foliage. Could this be interpreted to mean that Corot had done his trees with the tips of his fingers? The dealer was prompt in his denial, saying that he had once seen Corot painting and that he had used a bit of cloth on a stick instead of a brush.

Some time afterward, business took me to the Japanese Embassy in Washington, where I met Professor Yukio Yashiro of the Imperial Academy of Art in Tokio and was taken on a personally conducted tour of the marvelous collection of Japanese paintings which was then in the Embassy. (This was before the Second World War.) We paused before a picture by Taigon (I think that was the name) who, Professor Yashiro told me, was then the greatest living painter in the Far East. This led to a discussion of techniques of various artists. He explained that any trick or device in applying paint was considered perfectly proper in his part of the world. Taigon, he said, frequently used the handle of his brush with very telling effect.

My next source of inspiration came from an unknown woman who was copying pictures in the National Gallery of Art in Washington. She expressed the opinion that Renoir had used something like a bit of cloth to gain some of his silky effects.

Experimenting with cloth, I ultimately evolved what I call

the "bath-towel technique" of painting, and from that I evolved another method which I call the "toothbrush technique." By the former I can now paint grassy foregrounds that are soft (see Fig. 15, between pages 92 and 93). You will, I hope, feel in this picture that your foot would sink down into soft, yielding grass that would neither cut your shoes nor spike your ankles. I cannot guarantee that my methods are the same as Renoir's or Corot's, but, for whatever it is worth, I give them to you.

THE BATH-TOWEL TECHNIQUE

This method consists essentially of blurring the fresh paint with a bit of coarse bath towel. First I paint my foreground in a mosaic pattern, such as you see in some of Cézanne's pictures and other works in the Impressionistic manner. This consists of applying short strokes (horizontal if the land is level and slanting if the land slopes) of variegated colors to the canvas. The colors are so chosen that the optical blending as seen from a distance gives the desired effect. They must have a somewhat stronger Chroma, however, than would be the case if nothing further were to be done to them. (See Fig. 15, between pages 92 and 93.)

Next I take a small strip of bath towel, about 1 inch wide and 2 or 3 inches long, and roll it into a small tight cylinder about the size of the last two joints of my little finger.

The next step needs to be done with extreme care and deliberation. Taking the small roll between my thumb and forefinger, with the axis of the roll in a horizontal position, I brush the wet paint lightly with an *upward* swaying stroke, moving it barely in contact with the wet paint, not over an inch each time. Usually a stroke is somewhat shorter.

I never make more than one stroke with the same spot on

the towel. Before making a second stroke, I turn the roll so that a fresh clean place is available and then repeat. I keep on turning it, unrolling and rerolling it to find clean places until the job is done. If I forget and rub the picture twice with the same spot, the paint smears as if I had rubbed a finger over it. If this occurs, I scrape off the paint with a smooth-edged grapefruit knife, then repaint, and use the towel again.

In this treatment of foreground grass, it is important that the bath-towel technique should be carried from the top downward, rather than vice versa, although you always brush upwards. In other words, you paint from back to front. This is done so that the tips of the grass are not cut off by successive strokes of the towel.

While this method of producing soft grass is very satisfactory, it requires a consistent handling of other parts of the picture. Frankly, I have not yet been able to develop an equally satisfactory method for painting tree foliage. For if grass is woollike in its softness, it would seem that tree foliage should possess a somewhat comparable texture. Rugged tree foliage and silky grass do not seem to belong in the same landscape.

The Toothbrush Technique

While experimenting with the towel method I also tried using an old toothbrush after bending the handle nearly at right angles with the bristle holder. Plastic handles are easily bent by heating them with a burning match, but you must be careful to avoid setting fire to the flammable plastic material. (Bone handles cannot be bent in this way.) The toothbrush makes a much coarser brushing material than the bath towel, but the principle of its use is identical.

Each time the toothbrush is applied to the wet paint it must be wiped clean with a clean cloth wet with clean turpentine.

Up to now my experiments have revealed that this technique is more suitable for reeds and rushes than for grass or hay. It has proved very satisfactory for depicting a bramble patch beside an old stone building (see Fig. 15), and once I felt that the tooth-brush method of rendering trees in an autumn gale or a droop-ing willow was far better than the orthodox brushing technique (see Fig. 16, between pages 92 and 93).

We must always remember, however, that such devices as these, although interesting and helpful, are only a substitute for real skill in handling an ordinary paintbrush.

OTHER TRICK METHODS

Another painting device, which I discovered quite by acci-dent, is that of carefully scraping off a picture after it has been painted. One picture I painted was so poor that, after I had completed covering a 16-by-20 panel, I decided to scrape it off and go home. Just why I began scraping with the palette knife in a systematic manner, beginning from top down in vertical strokes, I do not know. At any rate, that was a procedure which left a little paint in the interstices between the threads of the canvas. The effect was a rather pleasing landscape, looking as if it had been viewed through a mist (see Fig. 17, between pages 92 and 93).

Art is full of strange surprises.

My advice to beginners is to stick to orthodox painting for the first two hundred pictures. As in all human endeavors, it is advisable to learn the usual way of doing a thing and their limi-tations before adopting the innovations. The towel and tooth-brush were pressed into use merely because I felt that it was impossible to get the desired results any other way.

~~~~~~

TEN

Care of Brushes

YOUR MOST important tools are your brushes—and they are the most easily ruined by lack of proper care. Since they cost from about 40 cents each up to about $2 for bristle brushes and about $5 for Russian sables, you may have approximately $25 worth of this equipment. It can be rendered nearly useless by carelessness.

Most of the troubles that occur with brushes are due to paint drying in the bristles. The remedy, of course, is to keep them clean between jobs. Whenever I stop a day's work, I wash my brushes clean with turpentine, wipe them dry on a towel, and put them into my box. By the time the next painting day comes around they are stiff, for the turpentine has evaporated, leaving a gummy residue around the bristles. When next I want to use them I dip the bristles into clean turpentine, and in a moment they are soft and pliable again.

Some writers and many artists insist that brushes should be washed with soap and water before they are put away. I have done that, too, but it takes time, and time is the scarcest thing in my life. I would rather be painting than washing brushes when business cares permit me any time for my avocation.

If you want to wash your brushes, this is the way to do it. First, get out all the color by washing in turpentine; then wash out all the turpentine by using soap and water. It's a bit messy, so don't do it in your wife's bathroom, or you may wish you hadn't. Better do it in the kitchen sink or in the basement or the garage.

Procedure: Wipe the brush dry of turpentine after you have got out all the paint that is removable by this reagent. Then start a small stream of water. Wet the bristles, and rub them on a cake of laundry soap. Then rub the soapy bristles against the palm of your hand. Wash off the paint and turpentine with water. Soap the bristles again, and repeat the rubbing against the palm of your hand. Repeat this routine until you produce a lather. No lather will form as long as there is turpentine in the brush. Continue until the lather is white and no more color comes out of the bristles. Wash out the soap, and wipe the brush as dry as possible. The bristles will still be wet, and they must be dried out before you can use the brush again. Lay the brush flat somewhere near a window or a radiator for a few hours until it is thoroughly dry. Then you can put it away in your paint box and forget it for a long time, and it will stay as good as new.

Soap and water are good, but they are not my preference for brush cleaning. I prefer to use a paint remover, usually acetone. You can get it by the pint at your hardware or paint store. It is also sold as a brush cleaner, though generally at a somewhat higher price than when labeled as a paint remover.

This organic paint remover is very flammable, so don't allow smoking or open flames near by. For instance, don't use it in your kitchen where the pilot flame on the gas stove or gas refrigerator may cause it to ignite. I usually use it in my own bathroom and then use more of the cleaner to clean up any mess that I make.

Procedure: Pour about a ½ inch of the paint remover into a small dish or tin pan, such as an individual muffin tin. Stand the brushes up to be cleaned, with only their bristles dipping into the paint remover, for about two to five minutes. Remove, and wipe them on a towel. Then repeat with fresh paint remover, and keep on repeating until the brushes are clean. Wipe them as dry as you can and leave them somewhere to permit final evaporation of the last traces of the paint remover. This method permits the cleaning of several brushes at a time. If an occasion arises when you know you are going to leave your painting kit for a long time without using it, I recommend that you clean every brush in this manner.

Several words of precaution are needed, however. The paint remover is extremely flammable, so be very careful where you use it. It is also irritating to the skin, so keep it off your hands as much as possible. (It does not harm your skin, though, despite any itching you may experience.) If you spill paint remover on painted woodwork, varnished floors or furniture, or on any plastic material, you are in for grief. The idea is to take the paint out of the brush, not off the woodwork.

Some writers say that paint remover will ruin a paint brush by dissolving the cement in the ferrule that holds the brushes in place. Maybe so, but this has never happened to me, and I have nearly a hundred brushes in five or six different makes, ranging all the way from the cheapest sign-painter's brushes to the finest artist's brushes that money will buy. Perhaps the reason I have had no trouble is that I do the job very quickly, never spending more than four or five minutes cleaning each brush, followed by very prompt drying.

Another way of caring for brushes is to hang (not stand) them in kerosene. Many artists'-supply stores sell a gadget for this purpose (see Fig. 22) consisting of a wire frame over a glass dish that holds about ½ pint of kerosene. The wire frame has a stiff coiled wire stretched between two uprights. Brushes can be squeezed in between the coils in a position where the tips hang in the kerosene. They should hang, not stand, because their weight, if standing on the bristles, may cause the bristles to acquire a permanent curve. One advantage of this sort of brush holder is that any fresh paint in the brushes will soak out and the pigments will settle on the bottom of the receptacle. This

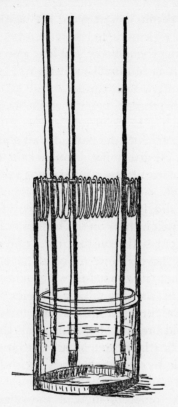

Fig. 22. Take Care of Your Brushes

Good brushes, especially sables, are expensive and easily ruined. A good way to preserve them is to suspend the brushes in kerosene in this gadget procurable at artist's supply stores. Never let any kind of brush rest on its tip!

saves cleaning. The disadvantages are that kerosene, being slightly volatile, has an odor; if spilled it is a nuisance to clean up; and, furthermore, the kerosene slowly evaporates from the receptacle. But kerosene is the best timesaver for the care of brushes.

Sable brushes require better care than bristle brushes. They are so much more expensive that extreme care is justified. I have found that washing them out in kerosene and hanging them in a brush holder is an eminently satisfactory way of cleaning them. But never allow their tips to rest on the bottom, or they may acquire a permanent bend that practically ruins them. Once, when I forgot to clean my favorite sable brush and it became hard and stiff with old paint, I used paint remover on it. No visible harm occurred, but I am not yet prepared to recommend this treatment as a regular thing for brushes costing several dollars each.

Spare brushes should be stood up in a jar with their *handles* down so that no weight rests on the bristles or hairs.

Brushes wear out with constant use and finally become so stubby that they have almost no utility. During the Second World War, when new brushes were almost unobtainable, someone discovered a way to salvage old ones. I have found this method to be partially successful in rejuvenating thirty-six out of thirty-seven old brushes of varying qualities. It depends on the fact that the bristles extend about 1 inch down into the ferrule. It is possible to remove about ¼ inch of the ferrule and have a brush that is nearly as good as a new one.

To remove the outer ¼ inch of the ferrule, use a three-cornered file to cut the metal down to the bristles. Then take a small pair of pliers and work the outer tip loose and remove it. You will probably find a lot of old dry paint in the bristles which can be removed with paint remover as previously described. You may also find that you need to use the scissors to trim the brush into proper shape.

Speaking of trimming brushes, the best advice I can give is: Go easy on this operation. In theory, at least, the tips of bristles are supposed to be the natural ends of growing bristles, not the cut ends. My one experience with a major operation of this sort

was on a Russian-sable water-color brush that cost me $7.50.
When I had completed barbering it, it was absolutely worth-
less. But water-color brushes are different from oil brushes.
Nevertheless, you have been warned.

ELEVEN

Choosing the Subject

WHAT TO PAINT

A KNOWLEDGE OF how to paint is good as far as it goes, but merely knowing technique—*how* to be a good craftsman—is a far cry from being an artist. For art is a method of communication of idea by line, color, and form. If there is no idea worthy of communication, there can be no good picture. In general, the worthy idea is one from which the artist himself gets some sort of emotion. The emotion may be a sense of pleasure at seeing an interesting landscape. It may be the charm of a venerable building or tree (for all things that are good are more interesting as they grow older). It may be a riot of autumn colors. Or it may be the homely feeling of familiar things. Anything that is a subject of a good painting is something that makes the artist *feel* an emotion. And without that emotion, the artist cannot communicate anything which will make a really worth-while picture.

Therefore, much depends on the artist's own capacity to react to a subject. This quality of reactability is also known as "temperament." Unless a painter possesses the capacity to feel an emotion to an extent far greater than his average fellow men, he will not be much of an artist. He will be a sketcher. He may have a heap of fun at his sketching, but he will often be at a loss to know what to paint because so few things will cause him to feel the emotion that results in a good picture.

The foregoing is my rationalization of my own experiences in trying to decide what to paint. It seems to me that good art is a subjective matter for which no amount of determination or will power can possibly act as a substitute. Either you *feel* like painting a good picture, or you do not paint one. As one artist once told another in my presence, "If you don't feel right, you can paint all day, and, no matter how hard you work, you can't produce anything but a bunch of 'tripe.'" The other readily agreed.

An understanding of the artist's psychology may be of value even to the self-taught beginner who is often at loss to know what to paint. He may spend the better part of a day looking for a good subject and then come home empty handed. I have done so myself. Occasionally, I have discovered that the good subject I was seeking was right at home within a minute's walk of my own door. Why hadn't I seen it in the morning when I went out? This is a question I have often asked myself and have not always answered satisfactorily. Two of the reasons that have occurred to me are these:

1. The light was different. The subject did not appeal to me in the morning light as it did in the late afternoon. That this reason is not wholly valid is shown to my own satisfaction by the fact that one of my better pictures, of a scene that I had passed up repeatedly, was done in the morning light (see Fig. 18, between pages 92 and 93).

2. I was weary and fagged out in the morning but became rested by a day of hunting for a suitable motive. This seems to me to be a sound reason, for I have observed that being out late at night is about the worst possible preparation for a successful painting—or any other sort of a day's work, for that matter.

One of the benefits which I believe might come from the aid of an art teacher would be the selection of good subjects for a picture, particularly when the beginner is at loss to know what to select. It is not uncommon for some of my friends and me to spend hours in search of a subject when, as a matter of fact, we might have been using those hours to paint or sketch. There is so little time available to the hobby painter.

When you are out with an accomplished artist it is usually wisest to let him choose the subject, for his experience will often detect a picture where you as a novice will see nothing. Sometimes the artist will allow the beginner to pick the subject, saying that he will find something to paint in the locality where the beginner feels he is inspired to do a job. I once was permitted to make such a choice for a professional. The scene was one I considered to be perfect, but his only comment was, "Too much scenery and not enough picture." But I was obdurate and insisted that this was what I wanted to do and went to it. In the course of the next few hours I made a color sketch that was wholly lacking in pictorial composition or ideas and was later consigned to the incinerator.

It would have been far better if I had asked the professional to pick out the picture to be painted, but perhaps I learned my lesson the better by doing it the hard way.

All that is pleasing or restful to the eye is not necessarily a picture. Back in the days when I was using only a camera to capture landscapes I was often importuned by well-meaning friends to shoot hillsides of green trees, but when these were printed in black and white they showed absolutely nothing of interest. Many people have taken photographs from high places, such as a mountaintop, and later been disappointed because they have not obtained pictures.

I once heard a talk by Adolph Fassbender on "What to Photograph," in which he said that "good pictures are close by, not far away." That same principle holds good in painting pictures from nature. I do not mean to discourage you from painting vistas; I merely want to point out that a vista is only a part, and should not be the whole, of a composition. There must be a bal-

ance between what is near and what is far, as well as balance in
the composition of the elements that are near by. Thus a good
picture has two-way balance, of composition: sideways and
from front to back.

The city man seeking a landscape subject in the near-by
countryside is often handicapped by the very thickness of the
population. For around nearly all cities there are beautiful sub-
urbs, but they are usually fenced in or have signs warning off
trespassers; or there is no place where he can leave his car; or
the fences are so close to the road that stopping is impossible
without blocking the highway. Furthermore, in the East, where
I live, there is so much landscape gardening and so many high
hedges that it is well-nigh impossible to find a satisfying subject
within a reasonable distance of home. This leaves me the choice
either of driving a long way or of working from a subject that is
right at hand—one so familiar from daily observation that it
lacks the novelty that inspires me to do good work. Hence I
must often paint in the Bronx River Parkway where there are
constant passers-by who sometimes annoy and often disturb by
uninteresting questions.

There was the time when I set up my easel in a railroad yard
with the idea of doing something in the Modernistic manner.
On this occasion (during the Second World War) the police
chased me out because there was a security regulation that pro-
hibited painting, sketching, or photographing a railroad bridge.
It was fortunate that I was not arrested, but the vigorous questioning by the cop aroused my anger to such a point that my picture was no good.

Tree landscapes are difficult to find in places where the trees
grow so close together that you cannot distinguish the border
of one from another. If the trees are not too close, you may be
able to omit many of them and develop a satisfactory composi-

tion. The simplified sort of landscape that I so much admire I
discovered, after a ten-year search, does not exist anywhere except in the imagination of the artist.

I like to paint old and weather-beaten buildings. Antiquity
lends them a charm they never possessed when new. One of my
friends ribs me a great deal for including a building of some
kind in almost all my pictures. But I have a feeling that without
this building something is lacking in my composition. There
seems to be a rational explanation for my feeling. A human figure is the most interesting subject for a picture, whether the
picture be a portrait, a figure painting, or a landscape with one or
more figures in it. But the next most interesting subject matter is
a work of man. Even footprints in the snow add something to a
snow landscape that would otherwise be lacking. The tip of a
chimney or a bit of roof showing over a hill, a path running
through a wood or field are all in this category. A seaside picture
is usually more satisfying if it includes a figure, figures, or some
man-made object like a pier, an old boat, old piles, dolphins
(posts—not fish) or the like.

A few years ago a *New Yorker* cover showed a group of summer artists getting ready to exhibit their summer's work. Everywhere it brought forth gales of laughter because each picture
was a green landscape with a red barn in it. I mention this because it answers the old question, "Why paint the old red
barn?"

To me the answer is simple. The Week-end Painter usually
finds nothing but green in his summer landscape, the monotony
of green being most prominent in the month of June in the
Northern Hemisphere. Such monotony, which is the result of a
single color, is very difficult to make into a satisfying picture.
Arthur S. Allen has said that the normal eye automatically seeks
a 5-value gray. By this he means that in an eye-satisfying room or
picture the combination of colors, if blended optically, will pro-

duce a 5-value gray. If any color predominates, the eye seems to sense the absence of the missing complementary color.

Now apply this principle to the landscape—or to a fragment or portion of the landscape—in midsummer. All about is green —grass, trees, shrubbery, gardens. Though green is restful to the eye, it needs other colors to complement or offset it in a painting. Since red is the complement of green, it is only natural that the old red barn or shed will add something of satisfaction aside from its function as an element of the composition. Reddish soil, brown rocks, red flowers, even dusty roads all possess to a greater or lesser degree the same sort of color contrast to this predominant green.

Thus if you want to put red objects into a green landscape, there is a scientific reason for doing so, and you shouldn't let ridicule deter you from doing what you *feel* is desirable. Red occurs very seldom in nature except in the spring and autumn or in far-western rocks and deserts. From the viewpoint of the *artist seeking contrasts out of doors,* June in the United States is usually the poorest month of all, despite the poet's saying. July is often nearly as lacking in differentiation of color, particularly a July that has had much rain. In August the color of the trees begins to change, many of them assuming yellow-greens, while others take on a brownish green suggestive of the autumn colors that will appear in the months to come. Fields and grasses may also assume new Hues, though where I live the small grain and hay fields are usually ripe in June or July.

September in my climate sees further changes, or differentiation, in the greens, but the real autumn colors seldom begin to show up until October. September produces lots of yellows, especially goldenrod. In October, however, comes the riot of colors that makes one want to paint every day while it lasts. November sees the falling of the leaves, but there is still color, other than green, in the landscape, for there are dead leaves on the ground, and most oak trees hold their brown leaves until late winter.

When the cold weather comes, the tendency is to paint indoors; but unless you venture out to study the winter landscape you will miss many colors that are only to be found in midwinter. I will admit that it is often a painful experience to paint outside in the cold; sometimes when the cold is intense the paint will not flow properly (water color will freeze on the paper). But there is much that satisfies in the winter landscape with its snows, its intensely blue shadows on a sunny day, its reddish stems of shrubs, its dead grass and weeds showing almost orange against the snow. It is well worth getting out to paint in the winter, provided you dress properly for the ordeal.

With the advent of the spring months, the contrasts of color begin to diminish, but there is no greater surprise for the beginner than the discovery that early spring landscapes have almost as much variety of color as autumn ones. As spring advances, the whole countryside becomes more uniformly green, reaching its maximum of green monotony in June.

The old red barn will always be a valuable inspiration in summer painting, but in other months it is less important.

Claude Monet partially solved the problem of what to paint by painting his own garden innumerable times, though of course he chose many other subjects as well. Your own back yard can afford you many a good picture if you will only study it with a certain degree of imagination. The basement door of the apartment where I live once afforded me a picture that was excellent save for a fault of composition; I failed to omit enough.

Waldo Peirce has made a great reputation by painting members of his immediate family. Most of his paintings were made in his own house.

Paul Cézanne painted landscapes around his home that are very satisfying to me. In fact, his at-home pictures please me more than some of his more famous landscapes, such as *Mont St. Victoire* or *L'Estaque.*

You do not need to go far afield to find a subject for a good picture. Just as good subjects are close to the beholder, so also there are good pictures near at home. There is the old saying, "The greenest fields are those which lie over the fence," and you should never forget it, especially when you find you are spending the entire day looking for a subject instead of actually painting. And in the journalistic world the saying is: "There are no uninteresting subjects, only uninteresting writers."

While it is true that a good subject for a picture is as likely to be found near one's home as far away, there is no denying the inspirational effect of a scene that is different. The landscape must inspire you to want to paint, yet after the same landscape has been painted time and time again it may cease to be a stimulant. Whether a given scene will inspire a good picture or not depends more on yourself and your imagination than on the scene.

Of course there are plenty of places that are "naturals." They contain a picture that is so obvious that even the novice cannot miss it. Such a scene is "Motive No. 1" at Rockport, Massachusetts, which has been painted so often that it has acquired that name. Indeed, professional artists who have maintained studios at Rockport tell me that this quaint old dock and one-time fish house is always the first thing anybody paints in the town, which abounds in hundreds of paintable motives. When I sketched there for the first time I knew nothing about the place or its art colony, yet after a quick look around I set up my easel and started on "Motive No. 1" (see Fig. 23), believing all the while that I had an unusually discerning eye.

There is one little observation, more interesting than useful, which I first made at Rockport: if passers-by merely glance hurriedly at your work without pausing, you may be sure that plenty of other artists have worked on the spot before you

Fig. 23. Popular Subjects

Some subjects are naturals for painting, such as this place in Rockport, Massachusetts. It has probably been painted more frequently than any other subject in America. Among artists it has earned the moniker "Motive No. 1."

showed up; also that it is probably a fairly popular scene to work on. The second time I noticed this absence of curiosity was in a small village on the west bank of the Hudson River some thirty miles above Manhattan. It is a place that is extremely difficult to reach but one whose quiet charm fairly cried out to be painted. Two small children sauntered over after I had been at work for a couple of hours, took a quick look, and then began to play catch. Later they came back for another quick look. Their lack of the usual curiosity prompted me to ask them, "Lots of artists paint here?"

"Oh, yes. Usually there are four or five every Saturday and Sunday."

Anyone who dislikes the endless routine questions of the casual passer-by will be gratified by the absence of comment in places where painting is regularly done.

There are other advantages, too. Where the population is accustomed to seeing artists at work, there is often a friendly attitude that permits you to set up your easel where otherwise it would be nothing but rank trespass. Plenty of times I have been driven off unimproved property where I never dreamed there would be any possible reason to object to my presence. Once I was working alone in a field on top of a hill in Connecticut, at least a mile from the road, when the owner drove in and invited me to clear out. So out I went, and the picture that was going so well has never been completed.

On another occasion I set up in a field just across the road from a quaint, very old cottage with wistaria vines in full bloom over the door. Pretty soon a tough old biddy came out and denounced me for trespass, saying that if I didn't move on she would call the State Police. "Ye dom'd artists! Ye make millions out of my poor little house. To Hell with the hull lot o' ye."

A professional artist recently told me of a place in New Hampshire where the farmers are very hostile to artists and drive them away with curses and threats.

Once I was doing a winter landscape, with my car parked back of me beside the road near where I had started work. Soon another car stopped alongside mine, then moved on to where I was working. The driver, an elderly man, remarked, "I suppose you do not realize that under that snow I have a nice piece of grass that I am trying to grow. You will have to move your car somewhere else." (This was way out in the country in the land of baronial estates.)

"Have you any suggestions as to where I can put it?"

"No—sorry. But you'll have to get it off my grass."

Alas, there was no other possible place within a mile, for the narrow road lay between rocky walls. Suddenly I had a bright idea.

"Wouldn't you like to invite me to run my car into your driveway?"

"Wouldn't I what . . . ?"

Just then his wife interfered. There was a hurried conversation in the car, after which she got out and walked over to me, saying, "Of course you can put your car in our drive. Please do. I paint, too."

And there have been other happy occasions, as once when a man came out of an elegant home near two of us who were hard at work on a very hot day. "I don't know a thing about painting," he said, "but I'll bet you chaps are thirsty. Would a little lemonade go well?" And he offered us a large pitcherful.

Another time a chap came out of a very poor little home bringing a cooling beverage without any of the preliminaries. All he said was, "I used to think I could be an artist. I know how hot it is when you are working for long hours. But now I am only a house painter."

A sympathetic attitude on the part of neighbors or onlookers helps a lot. But where there is suspicion and antagonism, it is impossible for me to paint. You might think that the latter would produce a picture in the manner of De Vlaminck, but his stormy scenes and ugly skies apparently do not come from anger.

WHAT NOT TO PAINT

Too often the painter fails to leave enough out of a scene to produce a pleasing landscape composition. A good picture is not a faithful copy of what one sees before him. Nature seldom produces a composition so perfect that it cannot be improved by man. This does not imply that man can make a better tree than nature, but man can sometimes arrange trees in a better way than the haphazard fall of seeds from other trees.

A very instructive exercise is to go to an art exhibition and study the composition of the landscapes. I once did this in Old Lyme, Connecticut, where one artist (Bicknell) had about a dozen small landscapes that appealed to me tremendously. I discovered that he seemed to have some sort of rule of composition whereby he limited each of his pictures to no more than ten elements. (For further discussion of elements see page 123. For twelve-element picture see Plate V.)

Since that time I have counted the elements in the compositions of other contemporary artists and, while few of them have so obvious a rule, I have found that the better ones are those who use the fewest elements in their compositions. You will almost never find in nature a landscape that even comes close to this desired simplicity. To attain it, your own imagination must tell you what to use and what to leave out. I do not recall that I ever saw a picture that was no good because it had too few elements in its composition, but I have seen hundreds that were far "too busy"—too full of superfluous things.

Painting a good picture is much like doing a good piece of writing. Every word, every sentence, every paragraph should be there for a definite purpose—never merely to fill up space. If any part of a literary composition fails to advance the idea that the author is trying to develop or impart to the reader, it has no business being there. Some novelists, even successful ones, clutter

up their pages with boring, superfluous descriptions, apparently
with the mistaken notion that they are creating "atmosphere."
Literary atmosphere has its place and, when well done, is very
important, but it is far better literary technique to create it by
more subtle means—in fact, to let the characters by their deeds
and words create atmosphere. When that is done you have
really good technique.

I believe that in pictorial composition there is a similar principle that the beginner should try to discover and, if he is satisfied with its merit, should try to apply in his own work. Probably
this is something that any art student would be taught in the
classroom, but, lacking that advantage, one must teach himself
by observation, thought, and experiment. Which of these three
is the most important to the self-taught beginner is impossible
for me to say; I believe that each is equally important.

Analysis of what an artist really does in painting a good picture is a very interesting experience; careful study may often reveal features in the work that the artist himself is not aware of.
He cannot tell you *why* they are there, for his instinct or sub-
conscious had prompted him to them. Professional critics have
a lot of fun doing this analytical work, especially those who lecture in art galleries and escort gaping crowds around the works
of the Old Masters, not only pointing out the obvious but call-
ing attention to tricks and devices which the artists probably
never consciously thought about. But what I am primarily concerned with here are those matters in pictorial composition in
which the artist must exert a conscious role, in which he creates
out of his own mind something that he wants to see on his canvas. It is where his *will*, not merely an accident, enters that I find
important.

The Japanese skill in arranging three flowers in a vase to
create a perfect effect is the sort of thing you must study if you

want to be a composer of good pictures. Whatever else we may condemn in the Japanese character, we must admit that they are past masters in the art of creating beauty out of a few simple elements.

While I am still on the subject of what to paint, there are a few other matters I should like to discuss. It was Corot, I think, who once said, "The finest pictures are painted in the studio." It may seem odd that it is easier to paint a fine landscape in the studio than out of doors, yet it has been my own experience that this is true. On several occasions I have attempted to do a 22-by-30 canvas out of doors, and I have never succeeded in producing a good one. I have had much better luck doing a smaller canvas on the spot and later converting my recorded impressions to a large picture in the studio.

There are several reasons for this. First of all, a big canvas takes too long to cover, unless perchance you can count on coming back to the same spot day after day at the same time. You can start a picture in the morning and work right through to sundown—maybe—but the scene before you changes every hour. In the afternoon it may bear almost no resemblance to the scene you started in the morning. Shadows reverse their directions; details appear where there have been none, and others disappear from places where they have been. It's a good thing to go through the experience *once*, just as it is a good thing to buy some shares in a worthless gold mine or wild-cat oil drilling venture *once* and in small amounts; also very early in your career. Then you won't make the same mistake again.

The second reason, which I consider more important, is the human tendency to paint in more details than are needed when working on a large canvas out of doors. Nature can produce more details than your imagination. If you work out a careful sketch outdoors and then use this as an idea for a bigger picture indoors, you will be aided by the absence of the multitude of needless trivia that clutter up a canvas without really forwarding the central idea you are developing.

In the studio your imagination can fill in much that you would like to see in a picture. You are not hampered by merely factual realities. And remember that you are not doing a colored photograph, you are *creating* a picture.

A third reason for not doing big pictures out of doors is a mechanical one. A big canvas on your easel is like a sail. Even a small gust of wind will tip it over. When this mishap occurs, you will find that it always falls "butter side down," and you will have the task of cleaning off a thousand bits of leaves and grass and other debris before you can resume painting, which is very conducive to language inappropriate for a Sunday.

If you were sent out by the editor of a publication to write a story about a busy factory, the probability is that you would fill a notebook with all sorts of accurate memoranda. And very likely you would make notes about the way the place reacted upon your senses. Perhaps there would be sunlit rooms, workers in spotless uniforms, smiles everywhere—a place where people were happy in their work. You would record such impressions in your notes. On the other hand, you might find a forbidding sort of place, with damp floors, smelly, with evil-looking, scowling workers, ill-tempered people who were constantly bickering and snarling at each other and perhaps doing their utmost to make everybody else unhappy. (I have seen factories just like that.) You would put all this down in your notes while the impression was fresh.

Then what would you do? Would you sit down, then and there, in the factory, to write the article or story, or would you go to a secluded spot and begin to think over what you had seen, arrange your ideas of what was most important, decide what unimportant material should be omitted? If you had any experience in writing, the latter course is the one you would invariably pursue. You would decide what the story was to bring out, what was to be the central theme; then you would subordinate all else to bringing out that theme.

Painting a picture in the studio should follow much the same procedure. The sketches you have made in the field are your notes, portraying not only the arrangement of objects but their form and color, their mood, their lights and darks. Some folks have the notion that it is well to keep on painting on the same picture after you get it home, but I do not. I would no more think of materially reworking a good outdoor sketch than I would of trying to write new notes on top of old ones in my notebook. The thing to do is start afresh, with a new canvas in your own studio, and try to improve on what you thought you saw.

To be sure, you may want to visit the old scene again to recapture some essential that escaped your pictorial note taking, just as a writer may find it necessary to revisit the place he is writing about to discover some of the essentials that, after due reflection, he realizes he has overlooked.

To summarize: You don't have to go far afield to find something to paint. By the process of subtracting the nonessentials from almost any scene you can create an interesting composition for a picture.

TWELVE

Painting the Picture

Now comes the actual painting of the picture. This is the real fun. You have taken your equipment out to a place that inspires you to want to paint a picture. You have your easel, paintbox, canvas panels, lunch, pipe or cigarettes, *and matches.* Nothing has been forgotten. You are probably out with one or more kindred souls who are equally well supplied with the essentials for a perfect day in the country. Perhaps you are alone.

Oddly enough, you do not often plunge right into the job at hand. First there must be considerable study and planning of just what you are going to paint and how you are going to paint it. I have been astonished at how much time a good professional artist will devote to the job of preliminary study. But, as I grow in painting experience, I find that I too am taking more time for these indispensable preliminaries.

The hobby painter is usually handicapped by the shortness of time at his disposal. A good oil sketch requires very little time for execution by an experienced painter after all the preliminary study has been successfully concluded. There was a time when I would need six to eight hours for a 16-by-20-inch sketch, which was too long for the light or time available. I can now do a sketch of this size in anything from two hours of actual painting time to four or five hours.

Make ample allowance for the time consumed by painting, for it is disappointing to be forced to quit before you are ready to do so by darkness, a train schedule, or promises to be home in time for a dinner appointment.

Furthermore, there is the problem of the angle of the sun's

rays, for the sun fairly races across the sky once you are profoundly interested in your work. Shadows reverse their direction as the sun passes midday, and the whole aspect of nature changes with startling speed and a contrast that is seldom observed or noted by those who are not artists. This will astonish and confuse the beginner until he learns to foresee the changes and allow for them in his calculations. A scene that was most attractive in midmorning may turn out to be rather flat and uninteresting as the day wears on. Or it may change into something wholly unexpected and better than the original—though generally it is worse. When the latter occurs you must have recourse to your memory of the time before the light changed, but this is not always reliable for it is very difficult to look at a scene and paint it the way it *was* and not the way it *is* now.

There is another problem caused by the passage of time when you are painting near the ocean: the movement of the tides. Many of the subjects that are most attractive to the artist are scenes around docks and fish piers or salt marshes. If you are going to do a worth-while sketch, there are certain parts of these scenes that you must complete at a desired stage of the tide. Time and tide wait for no artist. Ships that were afloat may be aground and over on their sides with masts at very different angles in half a day. Or the tilted, grounded ship may float vertically. Or that picturesque, abandoned old tugboat may be completely submerged and out of sight four hours after you have started to work.

Worse yet, though you may plan to come back the next day to continue that sketch which showed so much promise, the tide will not be the same, each stage being about an hour later on each succeeding day. You may then wait for the tide to be right and find that the light has changed. Shore scenes on tidal waters can seldom be duplicated exactly.

Ships come and go, regardless of the stage of the artist's work.

Once I thought I had foreseen everything when painting in an old shipyard; I was sure nothing could ever change there in any way that would disconcert me. Then a big black-hulled yacht was hauled up right in front of me, completely shutting off my subject. There was nothing to do but pack up and go home.

Also to be considered in your planning of your painting is the probable amount of sunlight that may fall on your canvas at a later hour in the day, when it will be too late to start another picture. It often happens that a nice shady place where you would like to set up your easel will be in brilliant sunlight two hours later. Or the cloudy day that permits you to work at will, regardless of sunlight and shadow, may unexpectedly clear up and change the whole scene, and the sun may shine so brilliantly on your canvas that it is impossible to work there any longer. A picture painted with brilliant sunlight falling directly on the canvas generally looks very flat when you take it indoors and view it by the subdued light of the interior of your home.

There have been times when a shaded position under a big tree has not been as satisfactory as I expected, however. When the tree is broad leafed, like a sycamore or a catalpa, the sun often penetrates the foliage to the extent that it throws a strong yellow-green light on the canvas, making it almost impossible to judge one's colors accurately.

Compositions—Simple and Busy

For years I have greatly admired the landscapes that, for lack of a better term, I shall describe as "simple" landscapes. By "simple" I mean that these pictures have very few elements in their composition; in each one there are only a few important objects. But where can one find such simple landscapes to paint?

This should be no problem at all to one who has received

competent art instruction. They exist only in the imagination of the artist. Bicknell, whose work is always pleasing, seldom used more than ten elements in a 12-by-16 canvas. By "element" I mean major area or major object. For my purposes the sky counts as one element, but if there is a huge cloud dominating the sky I call that another element. The foreground counts as one if there is no other object of great interest in it. If the foreground is cut in two pieces by a fence or a road, then it becomes two elements, and any other major object counts for another. I also score one each for human figures, houses or other buildings, trees or big rocks, and anything else that seems to be of sufficient interest to capture the attention.

This may be a mechanical way of going at it, but I justify it in the belief that unless there is some numerical count there can be no rational basis for judgment. One can *feel* that there are too many elements of interest in a picture, but, if so, how many are the right number?

All true artists adhere to the principle of simplicity, which is the keynote of good art. Whenever you see a picture with too many elements in its composition—a really "busy" picture— the chances are it is not a very good picture. The skill of the artist does, however, permit considerable latitude in the handling of a larger number of elements. Fine artists manage to group and subordinate objects in such a way that several as a group may count as only one major element. So this Rule of Ten is only a rough generalization for guidance and not for too strict observance. In looking over my own work, though, I find that the good-for-nothing pictures are generally those in which I have put too much (see Plate V for a conscious application of the rule).

All this leads up to the problem of what you are going to put into your picture now that you have found a suitable subject and have located a suitable place to work. You are faced with the necessity of omitting a great deal from the scene before you in order to compose a good picture from it. This may require an entire hour. I don't think I have ever seen a picture that has been harmed by the omission of too much, provided the elements that were utilized were used in their proper size and relationship. Admittedly, it is possible to paint the objects too small for the size of the canvas and thus produce a sense of emptiness in it which is as bad as a sense of busy-ness.

FINDERS

At this stage of your preparations you will need your finder (see Fig. 24). This is a rectangular piece of heavy cardboard with a rectangular hole in the center through which you view the scene and find what you want to include. The finder will shut out all the extraneous objects near your subject. Doubtless you will have the frequent experience of driving in your car and spotting a splendid place to work, only to find, when you get out, that it is not what you thought it was. This will be due, in part, to the fact that the car windows have acted as finders and have framed off a section of the landscape so that it caught your favorable attention; and, in part, to the fact that you were much higher above the ground when you were in the driver's seat than when you stood on the road.

While a poor finder is better than none, as long as it is a permanent piece of your equipment it should be made properly. You can even hold up your hands to simulate a rectangle (see Fig. 25), but this is useful only for the preliminaries, before you get down to serious composition.

A good finder should be cut from heavy, very stiff cardboard. A flimsy one that flutters in a breeze is an abomination; you will have problems enough without that vexation. It should be stiff enough so that you can hold it with one hand. When the hole is too large in proportion to the total area from which it is cut, the remaining cardboard may be of insufficient strength to provide the requisite stiffness. Therefore, use a piece that is big enough —perhaps the bottom of an 8½-by-11-inch tablet.

Fig. 24. The Finder Frames the Subject

Your finder is used to cut out or exclude extraneous material from your subject. It should be cut out of very stiff paper board, leaving enough material to give it rigidity. The opening should have the same proportions as your canvas.

Next, the size of the hole should be carefully planned so that the length and breadth are proportional to the dimensions of your canvas. You should have a finder for each size of canvas that you use out of doors, because the ratio of the sides of a 12-by-16 canvas is slightly different from that of a 16 by 20. I also like to have a finder with a hole the right size so that when

I look through it at my canvas, holding the finder against the near side of the bowl of my pipe, the inside of the finder hole exactly coincides with the outside of the canvas when I am standing close enough to the canvas in order to draw on it.

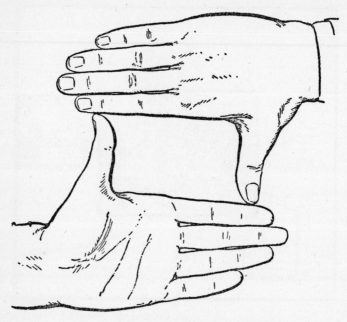

Fig. 25. Your Hands Can Be a Finder

For a quick study of a possible subject before opening up your painting kit, learn to use your two hands to form a rectangle as a substitute finder.

The benefit to be derived from this is that when I measure, say, the height of a tree through the finder by sighting at the handle of a paintbrush held at arm's length, the measurement bears a definite ratio to the canvas on which I am going to paint. And it is always the same ratio.

You will use a finder only at the outset, while the relation of the various elements of the composition is being determined. Once this relation has been settled, the finder will have little further use. But the method of measuring by holding the brush handle at arm's length should be continued until you are positive that everything is correctly drawn (see Fig. 26).

Fig. 26. Measuring

All set to begin drawing. The first step is to select a reference point, which in this subject could be the nearest corner of the house's foundation, and locate it properly on your canvas. Measure everything from that point. This chap is measuring the height of the building on a brush handle, but he will multiply all measurements by two in order to make his subject fill the canvas properly.

DRAWING THE PICTURE

While I am assuming that you know enough about drawing to sketch in the picture you propose to paint, I am going to add a few observations of my own. If you don't know how to draw, get some books on the subject and practice on paper. Drawing on canvas is not nearly so easy as drawing on a smoother surface that has no ridges to force your line off its proper direction.

Aside from the necessity of emphasizing certain characteristics of your subject, the need for accurate drawing cannot be overstated. This is where trained British artists excel. They are perfect. Charles Vezin, one of the Old Lyme, Connecticut, group of artists once told me, "You can't ever draw too well." Another artist put it, "You can never draw well enough." These admonitions are inserted here not to discourage you but to promote accuracy.

If your perspective is wrong and your buildings don't sit on the ground or if your roof lines are way off, it is because you have not measured your subject accurately. It is entirely possible to draw a good representation of a subject in a mechanical manner. If you will draw what you *see* and not permit what you think objects ought to look like to dominate your style, you will have very little trouble.

A good plan, where buildings are involved, is to select some reference point and measure everything from that point. Such a reference point may be the bottom of the nearest angle on a building or some other fixed spot that you won't forget easily (see Fig. 26).

MULTIPLYING FACTORS FOR DIMENSIONS

As you start measuring things at arm's length and then applying the measurements to the canvas you are apt to discover that everything is too small for the size of canvas. When this occurs there are two remedies: one is to move up closer to your subject; the other is to multiply your measurements by some factor like 2, 3, or 4. If you have used a camera a great deal, you well know that the image in your finder or on your ground glass grows larger as you move the camera nearer the subject. That is a common way by which the photographer enlarges a subject to make his composition fill the area properly. Another way open to him is to use a different lens. Some people even use telephoto lenses to bring their subjects optically closer without changing the character of the perspective. But, as an artist, you have to do things somewhat differently, for moving closer to your subject may, perchance, take you out of that nice shady place into a spot that will not be suitable for your work later in the day, or it may move you too close to the subject—so close that you are overwhelmed by unnecessary detail or the perspective introduces lines that you do not like. Hence the better plan is to multiply your arm's length measurements by some factor that will enlarge them to a size that will fill your canvas to your satisfaction.

Sometimes after a few preliminary measurements you may decide to erase the lines and start all over with a different factor. And sometimes you may decide that instead of a horizontal picture you will make a vertical picture.

DRAWING THE PICTURE

The drawing can be done with charcoal or with a pencil that is not too soft. I have found an ordinary No.-2 lead pencil to be satisfactory. I dislike charcoal, but many prefer it. A very soft pencil is to be avoided because the soft graphite smudges easily.

It is a good plan to cover each pencil line with a thin wash of cobalt blue and turpentine applied with a small round brush. Though desirable, this is not essential for small sketches. Working in the field with a small canvas permits you to take a few chances that you would never think of taking on a large canvas done in your studio. The big pictures painted in the studio are inspired by your sketches, which really are color notes. These

larger compositions are creatures of your imagination, supplemented by your observations recorded in smaller oil sketches.
When you do a large canvas, the general procedure is to draw in
the picture with charcoal or pencil and then always to cover up
the lines (see Fig. 19, between pages 92 and 93) either with
shellac or with a thin wash of turpentine and cobalt blue applied with a small round brush, taking care that the blue line
exactly coincides with the penciled line; otherwise the drawing
may be adversely altered. The lines must be covered to avoid the
dirtying of light colors when you begin painting.

Erasures can be made on canvas with an art-gum eraser, but
it is not advisable to erase too much on one spot lest the sizing
on the canvas be completely rubbed off.

Placing Objects in the Composition

Sometimes you will wish that an element that you want to include in your composition could be somewhere else in order to
satisfy your instinctive sense of a good, balanced composition.
In my earlier years of painting I once went out with a real artist
who is very robust—contrary to the popular belief that artists
are gentle souls with soft cultivated voices. "Is it permissible," I
called out to him where he was working about two hundred feet
away, "to move that tree over to the other side of the barn?"

"You're the artist!" he roared back—which I now know is
the only correct answer.

A common error for beginners when laying out a composition
is to make treetops come inside the confines of the canvas. I
used to do this all the time, and naturally all the other elements
were correspondingly smaller. My pictures didn't look right,
and I couldn't figure out why. One day a friend who knew good
art suggested that I experiment in my next sketch and allow the
tree to extend right up through the top of the canvas, with the

top edge cutting off the top half of the tree. I did, and the result was a great improvement.

Some of the conventions of composition seem to be pretty sound, especially that of never placing the horizon halfway up the canvas. A far better composition is obtained by placing the

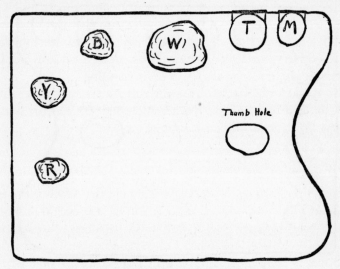

Fig. 27. The Simplest Possible Palette

You should start painting with only these colors until you are sure you know how to mix any color you think you need.
W = White; B = Winsor Blue; Y = Cadmium Yellow, Light; R = Alizarin Crimson; T = Turpentine; M = Medium

horizon above or below the middle. Nevertheless, some artists disregard this rule.

Now comes the question of how much detail to draw on the canvas. Some professional artists, I am told, draw in almost everything, and once I saw the beginning of a picture by an artist who always used this technique. The fact that he frequently sold his pictures for as much as six thousand dollars should lend a certain reverence to his method of work. A member of his family told me that he was very contemptuous of any artist who did not draw his picture completely before he began to paint. On the other hand, many good artists draw in only the major objects.

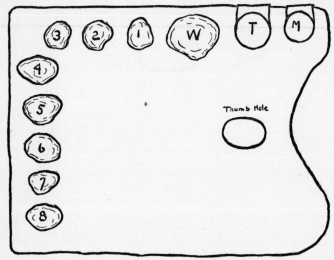

Fig. 28. A More Advanced Palette

The time soon comes when you need and can use more colors. W = White; T = Turpentine; M = Medium; 1 = Winsor Blue; 2 = Ultramarine; 3 = Cobalt Blue; 4 = Cadmium Yellow, Light; 5 = Yellow Ochre; 6 = Cadmium Orange; 7 = Payne's Gray; 8 = Alizarin Crimson

I have tried both ways and am in favor of less detailed drawing because otherwise so many of the details are covered by opaque paint long before I get to them.

LAYING THE PALETTE

We are now ready for the next step which, in artistic parlance, is called "laying the palette." This means putting fresh colors

Plate V. A TWELVE-ELEMENT LANDSCAPE

Here is a conscious effort to produce a very simple landscape from a very "busy" subje
It was started as a ten-element picture but ended up with twelve elements. In the act
subject there were five trees instead of two, also a bridge and a creek just this side
the trees. Houses on the distant hill were likewise eliminated. Elimination of noness
tials is important for good composition.

on the palette and getting it ready for painting. If you have never painted before, it is well to give some thought to how you want your colors arranged, for, once decided, you should always keep to the same plan. (You will find several suggestions for

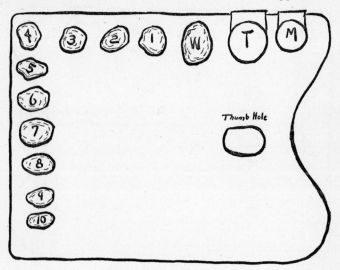

Fig. 29. A Larger Palette

You will want a further assortment of colors after a year or two of painting. Many colors, however, may crowd a 12- by 16-inch palette. Big assortments need bigger palettes.
W = White; T = Turpentine; M = Medium; 1 = Winsor Blue; 2 = Ultramarine; 3 = Cobalt Blue; 4 = Zinc Yellow; 5 = Cadmium Yellow, Light; 6 = Cadmium Orange, Light; 7 = Yellow Ochre; 8 = Payne's Gray; 9 = Burnt Sienna; 10 = Alizarin Crimson

palettes in Figs. 27–30.) This is desirable because you must be able to find the right color habitually in the same place and not make any mistakes. Every artist has his preferred arrangement, sometimes logical and sometimes quite illogical. I started out to be very logical, but as I added more colors to my palette I was forced to join the illogical painters rather than try to break habits of many years' standing. In general, however, it is wise to put white, the color you will use most frequently, in the place easiest to get at. My palette, shown in Fig. 30, is entirely satisfactory to me, with one exception. The bottom color of the left-

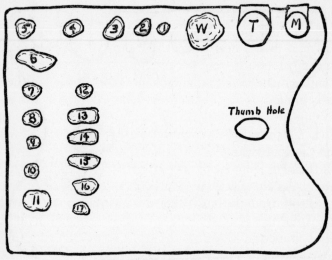

Fig. 30. My Own Palette

After twelve years of painting experience I have evolved this palette for my 16- x 20-inch painting kit.
W = White; T = Turpentine; M = Medium; 1 = Prussian Blue; 2 = Winsor Blue; 3 = French Ultramarine; 4 = Cobalt Blue, deep; 5 = Zinc Yellow; 6 = Hansa Yellow or Cadmium Yellow; 7 = Cadmium Orange; 8 = Payne's Gray; 9 = Lampblack; 10 = Cadmium Red, Light; 11 = Alizarin Crimson; 12 = Naples Yellow; 13 = Yellow Ochre; 14 = Raw Sienna; 15 = Burnt Sienna; 16 = Raw Umber; 17 = Burnt Umber

hand row is Alizarin Crimson, right where I always get it on my cuff if I happen to be wearing an overcoat in cold weather. And Alizarin Crimson is just about the most difficult color to remove from clothes. So, if you care to profit by the ruination of several of my garments, don't do as I do.

How Much Color

Don't be niggardly when laying out your colors; neither be extravagant. Only experience will tell you how much of one and how much of another to squeeze out. A self-taught lady once told me that she decided to take some lessons after she had struggled along alone for years. The frugality of her palette was anathema to her new teacher. He insisted that most of her problems stemmed from her parsimonious use of paint. Then he laid her palette out as he thought it should be, and the lady nearly fainted, for he had squeezed out as much as she would normally use in a month. But he was insistent that she use it all on a single picture. The results of his first lesson, she admitted, were very gratifying.

If the right color is not on your palette, the tendency will be to try to get along without it rather than take time to fetch the proper tube from the box. While it is wasteful to be extravagant with paint, it is also wasteful not to have enough paint to do the job properly.

After laying the palette, the turpentine and medium cups should be filled about one-third full.

Holding the Palette

Although the palette is designed to be held in the left hand, the weight of it nearly always gives me painful semiparalysis of the thumb. And in a breeze it flops about a great deal. It is absurd to hold a heavy palette all day. One's strength and attention can be much better applied to the job of painting the picture. So I have devised a method of getting away from the useless burden of a 16-by-20 palette; I use a water-color easel to hold it. The idea is recommended to you if you don't mind carrying the extra load when you go out on foot. In Fig. 13, between pages 92 and 93, you can see the setup.

One of my painting partners, after years of disdain for my lazy man's way, finally worked out a trick device that serves equally well. He fashioned a shelf which fits between the two front legs of his easel and now sets his palette on that.

Professional artists usually use painting tables in their studios rather than palettes. A painting table is merely a table with a smooth top of porcelain or plate glass on which the colors are placed and mixed. Some artists of renown use ordinary porcelain-topped kitchen tables for this work.

PUTTING ON THE PAINT

The time has now come to start painting. Most of what I can tell you about mixing colors and about brushwork has been described in earlier chapters. Therefore none of it will be repeated here.

In a limited sense, painting with oils is only drawing with oils. The better you can draw with a pencil, the better you can draw with a brush. This is a generalization, of course, for there is much more to actual painting than mere drawing.

Where to begin and *how* to begin are the two main problems that now confront us. The tendency of the beginner is to apply paint to the upper left-hand corner of the canvas and proceed right across the canvas as if he were writing. Sometimes this is proper, but sometimes it is better to follow a different procedure.

ESTABLISHING THE LIMITS OF VALUE AND CHROMA

In your preliminary studies of your subject you have noted where the lightest and darkest areas are located and also the places where the strongest and grayest colors are to be found. When starting to paint, you should spend considerable time reassessing these extremes. Then paint them in, first of all, before you paint anything else. This principle applies to whatever place on the canvas they happen to come. I think it is a great mistake for a beginner to start painting the sky until these limits have been carefully established. The reason for this is that the inexperienced painter has a tendency to get the sky much too dark. Usually, though not always, the sky is the lightest area in a landscape. Therefore everything else in the scene will usually be of lower Value. Hence, if the sky is started with a Value as low as 7 or 8, which is not uncommon for beginners, everything else must be of still lower Value. So if you start your sky too dark, you are licked at the outset. The picture will be dark and somber even when you are painting from a really brilliantly lighted subject.

At this point I want to digress for a few paragraphs to discuss light and its representation on canvas, borrowing some ideas I have learned from photographic studies (see Fig. 12, page 79).

The range of light intensity existing in nature on an average sunny day can easily be measured by the light meter which every owner of a good camera should always carry with him. On an ordinary day, neither brilliant nor gray, the light from the sky will measure from 65 to about 200 foot-candles. When it reaches 300, the day is very clear, and the illumination is very brilliant indeed. I have seen some skies that measure 700 to 1,000 foot-candles—and this is blue sky without the sun's rays striking the lens of the light meter. The light in the shadows under trees and bushes on the ground will sometimes measure only 1 or 2 foot-candles on a day when the blue sky measures perhaps a hundred times as much. The person who is not experienced in the use of modern photographic aids is usually unaware of these extreme contrasts. But the camera reveals the difference, if the photographer has not allowed for it in his lens aperture and shutter speed, by shadows that are black and devoid of detail.

The reason the human eye usually fails to register these great contrasts is that the eye possesses an automatically adjusting lens and aperture, the iris.

In making a photographic print from a negative that has been obtained by correct exposure of the film to a scene that has a 200 sky-reading and a 2 shadow-reading, we are compressing these true light readings to reflected light readings, the reflections being from the paper. These reflected readings are greatly limited by the very nature of things and afford much smaller contrasts than the original light readings—from 0 to 10 as compared to perhaps 1 to 200. The light reflected from any object, other than highly polished, light-colored metal, is always considerably less than the light that falls on the object. Therefore the photograph records contrasts that are generally less than one-fourth of the actual contrasts of the scene photographed. And when I say "contrasts," I refer to the lights and darks and the manner in which they affect your sense of vision. For anyone who is really trying to master the technique of painting, a complete understanding of this principle is desirable.

Painting in oils, water colors, or pastels is subject to the same limitations as photography when it comes to the representation of light and dark. For we view both photographs and paintings by reflected light. Nevertheless, there is a Russian painter who is said to have used luminous materials in his paints to get away from these limitations. His pictures are remarkable for the light that seems to come from them, but his dealer in New York emphatically denies the "slanderous tale" of luminous materials.

There is no conflict between the Munsell Scale of Values and the measurements of light reflected from the painted surface of a canvas. Munsell Values are an index of the contrast between the reflected lights and darks, from paper or canvas, whereas light-meter readings are absolute physical measurements that vary according to the strength of the incident light, that is, the strength of the light source.

Now, applying all this to painting: if the maximum possible contrasts between light and dark in a painting is only a quarter of that observed in nature, you can readily see that, if you paint the lightest part of your picture at, say, 7 Value, you are greatly limiting yourself, for you will then have available only about two-thirds of the maximum possible contrast between white (Value 10) and black (Value 0). Actually the limitation is even greater because this lowest possible Value is seldom used.

If my exposition is clear and you are able to apply it, you will have achieved in a very short time what it took me about eight years to figure out. There came a time when, to borrow a simile from music, I realized that I had been playing on only about three octaves of the piano when I had available the whole range from 0 to 10. I found out later that I was likewise restricting myself to a very few units on the Chroma scale. The net result was that most of the pictures I painted a few years ago are insipid and uninspiring. The fault stemmed from my lack of knowledge and lack of color courage.

Therefore, if you follow my suggestions as to procedure in painting, you will paint on a few spots of color here and there which will represent the maximum and minimum of Values and Chromas in your subject, leaving the keynote color of the sky until you have finished these preliminaries. The reason for leaving the sky to the last is that it is very difficult to mix a light enough sky color when working out of doors. Many a time a sky color that seems almost white when on your palette turns out to be too blue and too dark when viewed indoors. When I paint the other reference colors first, I am forcing myself to make my sky color much lighter than I used to do when I began in the upper left-hand corner as if I were writing on a sheet of paper.

There is nothing sacred about these reference colors. Their

only purpose is to compel you to utilize the whole gamut of Chromas and Values available by staking out what appear to be the limits in a given scene or subject. If, after trying to paint within these limitations, you find that your limits are too wide (I don't believe you will ever find them too narrow), it is comparatively easy to correct them.

My justification for spending so much time on this general idea is that my own painting made a big jump in quality as soon as I realized it. The notion came to me one night during the Second World War when I listened to a radio interview of an aviator who had just sunk a Japanese cruiser. He had a marvelous story to tell, but he was "mike shy" and told his tale in a colorless monotone, while the voice that interviewed him was forceful and beautifully modulated. Though the interviewer had no such story to tell, he had a voice that was intrinsically more interesting. It had contrasts of quality and intensity of tone. Why not apply this principle to painting, I thought, and the next day I tried to. The effect was a 50 per cent improvement in my painting.

In painting, what you have to say should be said clearly and vigorously by the use of colors and light and shade. You discover this fact soon enough when one of your efforts is viewed in an exhibition, particularly when it is in competition with the works of professional artists of considerable attainment. Just as you could not expect to make anyone hear you in a crowd if you spoke in a very weak voice, devoid of expression, you cannot make anyone hear or see what you have to say unless you present your pictorial ideas with emphasis.

I particularly dislike the method of painting which I describe as "sneaking up on it" by a slow and gradual process. This consists of putting on one color that is not right, then covering it with another color that is better, and repeating the painful approach until the right color is attained. Frequently the color becomes extremely muddied in this laborious attempt. Why not put on the proper paint the first time?

The answer to this question is, I think, a psychological one. The "sneaker-upper" is not bold. His caution does not permit him to use full-strength color where it is needed. The greatest handicap of the "sneak" method is that it often results in over-neutralized colors. It must not be forgotten that an inexperienced painter can seldom lay one color over another wet color without mixing in some of the lower layer. This not only makes for muddy colors; it also usually weakens the Chroma. Chroma cannot be increased by admixture; Chroma always loses strength when colors are mixed.

Another thing: although oil colors are not subject to the limitations of water colors, an oil painting that is done correctly at the outset always appears to be cleaner and fresher than one that has been worked over and over, unless the paint has been allowed to dry between the several paintings

To be sure, you can be a sneaker-upper, if you choose. But why not be courageous from the start? So, having put in the color reference points in their appropriate places on the canvas, the next step is to proceed with the painting of the whole picture.

Get the entire canvas covered with color that is as nearly correct as you can make it without stopping to finish one part before you go on to the next. Then step back and look it over critically, or get one of your painting partners to give you his criticism. After that, go to work to correct the faults.

There may be places that ought to be scraped off and done over. If so, do not hesitate to go after them, even when a major operation is needed.

One rule of a professional artist is this: "When you get the canvas covered, that is when you *begin painting!*" With the beginner, however, that is often the time at which he feels that he has gone as far as he can.

Sometimes further painting will not improve a picture but will cause it to go backward. There is an old saying that every artist ought to have someone to tell him when to quit, when to stop further work, pack up, and go home.

It seems to me, however, that a picture starts to go backward when the painter becomes fatigued and loses his enthusiasm. Painting is hard mental work, requiring the most intense concentration which, though willingly given to your hobby, will tell on your energy in a few hours. You put so much of yourself into the job that you are worn out at the end of a day. When fatigue of this sort overtakes you, that is the time when a picture does not improve with further effort.

Stand Up or Sit Down?

Should you paint in the standing position, or should you sit? The answer seems to be to use the way that produces the best results for you. I have tried both ways for years and have adopted standing up for several reasons. First, a stool or chair is one more thing to carry; second, I have to get up out of a chair so frequently to walk back to view my own progress from a distance that the chair is a nuisance; third, I find that I do better work standing up; and, fourth, the exercise of standing up is good for a sedentary worker.

Working from "Back to Front"

It seems that almost everybody has, at some time in his life, done a little painting in water color. If you are one of this group, perhaps you will have acquired certain techniques in the use of that medium that are not equally applicable to painting in oils. Water colors, being very transparent, cannot be laid over each other, as is possible with opaque oil colors, without the under color showing through as well as darkening the combination. This darkening occurs because the only white available to the water colorist is the white of the paper shining through the paint. If the paint is thickened by successive applications of water color, the white of the paper is progressively obscured, resulting in darker Values (and muddiness). For this reason many water colorists have developed the technique of painting from "front to back," that is, painting in most of the things that appear in the foreground and then painting in the background after suitable drying time has elapsed.

The same painting method can be used in oils, but it is wholly unnecessary because oil colors are opaque and can be piled on each other as much as needed, provided the under paint is not mixed with the topmost layer. This permits you to reverse the water-color method and paint from "back to front."

I have found this to be a very useful way of doing a picture because of the difficulty of putting in small bits of background between near-by objects without undoing some of the more careful work in the foreground. Such things are bits of sky seen through the foliage of trees or anything that is seen through objects that are near to the painter.

A truly skillful artist will probably scoff at my method, although I have found it so helpful. Some professionals are able to paint "sky holes" in tree foliage without making the trees appear as if artillery shells had torn through them. Every painter develops his own method of doing things, which is the reason why the work of different artists painting from the same subject will differ so much in technique as well as ideas portrayed.

Avoid Radiating Lines

One common fault to be avoided is the use of lines that radiate where they should not. This error sometimes creeps into the work of quite good artists. It is most frequently observed in large pictures where there are many vertical lines, such as trees or buildings, which seem to radiate from a point several feet below the canvas. How it occurs is understandable enough. Many painters sit down to draw their picture on the canvas panel. On a small panel it is not very difficult to make the vertical lines parallel, but when a larger one is done in this manner the artist's eye plays tricks on him. It is later discovered that the vertical lines are farther apart at the top of the canvas than at the bottom.

The remedy is to place the canvas in a vertical position and criticize it from this viewpoint before many details have been drawn in. The best artists never seem to fall into the radiation error, but some who are not quite tops do, though they seem to get away with it, perhaps under the guise of Modernism or "tension."

How One Color Influences Another

It is possible to make a color on the canvas appear wholly different without so much as touching it by making changes in the adjacent colors, particularly when one of these is approximately the complementary hue. This is more pronounced when the colors are of strong Chroma than when they are grayed. I faced the phenomenon for the first time on a 24-by-30 landscape of a French village, where my red-tile roofs simply would not take on the color of old weather-beaten tiles. After weeks of painting and repainting I finally took it to an experienced artist for suggestions as to how to overcome the difficulty. She took only ten minutes to find the answer: "If you can persuade yourself to give up those intensely purple shadows beside the houses, I think you will have no trouble getting the roof colors you want." But how I hated to abandon those purples! To me, they were very hot stuff. Finally the purple shadows were grayed, and the roofs assumed the very color I wanted. In fact, they had been the right color all along, but I had been unaware of how the contrasting colors had modified their appearance.

It is in matters of this sort that expert instruction is very important. Nevertheless, once when working wholly on my own I discovered how to make an old, nearly black shingle roof appear as if the sun were shining on it. Hours of effort had failed to produce the effect I wanted, until I realized that if I did not hurry up and complete the sketch darkness would overtake me. As soon as I painted the shadow of the chimney falling across the roof, the whole aspect of the shingles changed, and the sun really shone on them. You can get quite a kick out of discoveries like this.

LOCAL COLOR

You will read and hear much about "local color," not only in landscapes but in all forms of painting. The term describes the color that is reflected onto objects from other colored objects in the vicinity. To me it has always sounded like a misnomer, for the blue sky or any other source of colored light will affect the color of anything on which such colored light impinges. If there is any doubt in your mind that reflections of color from certain objects are to be found on other objects, all you need to do is study the colors on the shady side of a white house. I suggest a white house because the reflected, so-called "local color" is more easily seen on a white surface than a colored one. It will be found to reflect a wide variety of Hues whose sources you can usually trace. To be sure, the local colors will be very faint until by long experience your eyes have become accustomed to seeing what is actually there.

In landscape painting there are few things more difficult to paint properly than a white building because of the variegated play of local color on all its surfaces. It is never really white. When the sky is blue, the shady side will be a light blue unless the reflection from grass, bushes, trees, flowers, and the like overpowers the sky reflection.

The rule is that if you yourself can see a colored object any other object in reasonably close proximity, regardless of its own color, can also "see" the same color—or could see it if it had eyes. The only possible way in which color can be seen is by the presence of colored light. And nature is full of colored light falling on every object that is not obscured by some intervening object.

All this is of importance in painting because a satisfactory representation of nature cannot be produced by giving objects their single direct color; the local color must also be included. To omit it is equivalent to omitting the overtones in a musical sound: it doesn't sound right.

The term "local color" has never seemed to be as appropriate as "reflected color" or "secondary color," but I shall not quarrel over a trivial point.

Local color is there in your subject or motive for painting, whether you are actually able to discern it or not. One very good artist used to tell his son to paint in the local color, even when he could not actually see it, and add that, if he would paint it in, the picture would be better than if it were left out.

In general, the lighter the Value of an object receiving reflected local color, the more pronounced that color will be. Darker objects, such as the trunks of trees, will not show local color so plainly. Also, the smoother the object receiving local color, the more clearly it will be shown, polished or shiny or even wet surfaces showing the most of all. Indeed, the only way that a wet asphalt pavement can be shown to be wet in a painting is by the reflections from it which, of course, are nothing but local color reflected to a very considerable extent, or percentage, of the incident light.

Reflections on water are but an extreme case of local color that has been largely reflected into the eye of the beholder. At midday the percentage of the reflected light is very high. At evening or early morning the percentage is lower. My own measurements with a light meter show that in the latter case about 50 per cent of the light is reflected directly from the original object. Therefore the reflections have half Value of the object reflected.

The French Impressionists whom I admire so much were the first artists to observe and actually paint local colors into landscapes.

There are two ways to handle local color in painting a picture. One way—and this method has a huge number of adherents—is to *mix* into the paint the color that represents the local color; here the blending is what I term "physical blending." The other way is to place the local color carefully on top of the normal color of the object, taking care that the local color is of the proper Value and Chroma. In placing it on top, it is not necessary to cover up the whole area. Frequently a few small, irregular spots of local color of the proper Value and Chroma will supply enough so that the eye of the beholder will not realize it is there but will be satisfied. This is what I term "optical blending."

Both methods are used by good artists, as you can see for yourself at any exhibition. My preference is for the optical blending of colors whenever it is possible.

One aspect of color has an important bearing on these principles. This is the relation of the area of a bit of color to the color perception of the person viewing it. One tiny spot of any color at about 5 Value on a large area of white or any other light color will usually appear as a dark *spot*, the color of which is indistinguishable. Enlarge that spot, and there will come a size when the Hue becomes apparent. If several spots of the same color are placed on the large white area, each separated from the other by about two inches, they will appear as so many spots, but if they are moved closer together they will begin to take on a color personality. You can utilize this phenomenon in your own pictures by putting in local color in small areas or even small dots. I have also used narrow streaks very effectively, such as a bit of ultramarine on the shady side of a tree trunk, in order to get the sky reflection and satisfy my eye without making the whole trunk dark blue.

If you choose to experiment with this method in your advanced painting, I counsel that you do not go in for the dotted technique of the Pointillists, who carried the idea to an extreme, nor to the larger variant of the same method that was developed by Georges Seurat. Though Seurat was a genius, a few of his pictures go a long way.

The advantage of studying these masters of the past is that you can discover how they worked and can adapt such of their methods as seem appropriate to your immediate needs. You should not merely imitate older artists.

CLEANING THE PALETTE

It is better to clean the palette in the field than at home. But if this necessary job has been neglected, it must be done as soon as you get in; otherwise the cleanup may be neglected so long that it will become triply difficult.

Unless you are painting every day there is no point in saving the paint on your palette for possible later use. It will dry out and have to be thrown away anyway. So the best procedure for the Week-end Painter is to scrape off all paint before going home. Then wipe the palette clean with a rag or piece of paper towel wet with turpentine. Next polish it with a dry cloth.

I have heard that some artists have a method of submerging their unused paints in water until they are needed again. This may be useful to one who is painting every day, but for weekly work it seems a bit cumbersome. And, of course, a *wooden* palette cannot be safely submerged in water, for it will split or warp.

PAINTING CLOTHS AND RAGS

From the very day you start to paint you will need a good supply of paint cloths. The most satisfactory type are old bath towels, which have excellent absorbent qualities. When people want to contribute to your hobby let them accumulate old bath towels for you. There is no more desirable gift. A good plan is to carry two cloths with you, one for wiping brushes and general cleaning up, the other for finally wiping your hands or removing paint from your garments.

Because of the rapid rate at which painting rags disappear, I have adopted paper towels as an excellent adjunct for wiping brushes and depositing the paint from my palette. They require but little room in the box and can be disposed of easily.

Never leave old paint rags on a farm. Animals have been known to eat them and die! The artist has to pay.

DATE YOUR WORK

Each picture you make should be dated with the month and year, whether you sign your name or not. It is surprising to see how many of your sketches will accumulate in a year, and after several years have elapsed you will frequently be unable to recall when you did them. This dating is for your own information—not for posterity. Every now and then it is a good idea to hold a private exhibition of your best efforts to determine whether you are going ahead or backward. Viewing your work chronologically, you will probably find that it is very irregular as to quality, yet you will often detect the beginning of trends that may be either bad or good. Sometimes a friend who is more advanced in painting will be able to point out where you have begun to introduce errors of technique that should be overcome before they become habits fixed by many years of application.

Framing Your Wet Pictures

A picture may be framed even if it is wet, provided you have suitable frames ready. A good plan is to have two or three gilt frames of the usual sizes, with holes drilled in their backs where nails may be easily inserted to hold the wet pictures in place. You can even have them equipped with picture wire so that your latest efforts may be immediately hung on the wall.

Summary of Procedure

In brief, the following are the steps you should take when you go out of doors to paint a landscape.

1. Take your equipment to the place where you expect to paint.

2. Study the subject and decide just what you are going to utilize in composing your picture. This may take as much as an hour.

3. Choose the spot where you are going to set up your easel for the next few hours.

4. Set up your easel.

5. Place a canvas panel on the easel.

6. Draw the outlines of the proposed picture on the canvas with either charcoal or pencil. Make the subject fill the canvas; in other words, paint it big—never small. Don't start painting until the drawing is satisfactory, especially as to perspective. Buildings must sit on the ground. Roads must be on the ground, not running up into the air. It is far easier to correct errors in drawing before you start to paint.

7. Lay your palette. Squeeze out a gob of each color on the palette. Clip on the turpentine cup, and fill it one-third full of turpentine. Ditto for the medium cup.

8. Mix a little cobalt blue with enough turpentine to make a thin wash. With a small round brush paint a dilute blue line over all your pencil or charcoal marks. This will leave a coating over the drawing that will not come off or darken lighter colors applied later. The turpentine will dry very rapidly.

9. Now start painting. Use a clean palette knife to take fresh colors from your various gobs for mixing. Always wipe the knife clean so as not to contaminate one color with another. Mix the colors on a clean place on the palette to the Hue, Value, and Chroma you want. Apply them to the canvas with a brush (or you can apply them with the knife). You are painting! This is where the real fun and the perplexities begin.

One way to paint is to put on your colors very thin, mixing them with considerable medium. The idea is to cover the canvas with thin color and then go over it a second time with thicker color (and less or no medium). My preference is to paint on the proper color directly.

10. Paint the darkest place first, then the very lightest. These will be areas of color by which you fix your limits of light and dark. Then paint the weakest Chroma color at its proper Value. Next, paint in the area having the strongest Chroma, or

strongest color, also at its proper Value. These will fix another pair of limits. Everything you do after this should come within these limits.

11. Step back ten or twenty feet at periodic intervals to get a more distant view of your work as it is progressing. You will wear a path in the grass.

12. When you are through painting, clean your palette and brushes. Put the picture into the paintbox. If you cannot paint again for another whole week, you may as well discard all the paint on your palette. By next Sunday it will be dry and hard and much more difficult to remove.

Sketches Are Not Studies

A SKETCH IN oils is a picture you make in a few hours on a small canvas, and it is done on the spot. In general, it is a series of notes in color about the composition inspired by the subject. From it you may produce another picture—a real studio painting which may take days of work for its completion. Some quick sketches, however, are often more pleasing than these labored efforts at home, for a sketch may have a spontaneity and freshness that cannot be recaptured in retrospect. (This is not to detract in any way from studio painting, nor to encourage slovenliness in making sketches.) However, as a rule, it is impossible to produce a really finished picture at one "sitting" before a subject. So you attempt to record only the essentials— what should be the basis of a good picture if time permitted you to complete it. This is the usual sketch.

A study, on the other hand, is a detailed picture of some small part of a subject. You make it for later use in painting another and usually larger picture. It comes pretty close to being a "portrait" of a detail, and certainly all the care and effort that goes into the painting of a human portrait should be expended on a study, for this is something you are going to keep and use later as a master copy when you are painting a big picture indoors. It may be a study of a cloud, a tree, a flower, an old shed, a piece of rusty farm equipment, an old boat, a bridge, or anything else that will remind you of the part in question when you are painting an important studio picture.

My first introduction to a study was not so happy as I now wish it had been. Long years before I ever dreamed of owning a

painting kit, a friend took me to call at an artist's studio in
Richmond, Indiana. In his racks he had a multitude of what he
called "studies" of beech trees, but nothing that he called a picture. When I asked the prices of these canvases, he merely said
they were studies and that he would have to paint me a picture
if I wanted one. But I wanted one of these; why not name the
price? He gently put me off, saying he would gladly paint me a
picture, the price depending on the size. Not having then the
slightest idea of the difference between a study and a picture
and without any enlightenment from him, I became annoyed
and walked out.

We were both in error. My ignorance prevented the kindly
old gentleman from making a sale; but he failed to realize I was
ignorant and therefore did not explain his unwillingness to sell
what really were his notebooks.

It seems to be impossible to make a painting that is both a
sketch and a study. Usually the study is as accurate a picture of
the detail as it is possible to make and as large as the canvas will
permit. When making a study, you are not interested in pictorial composition. Your purpose is to capture everything you can
see, so that at a later date it can take the place of the subject itself in your studio. If you can imagine having a whole tree in full
autumn colors in your own studio at whatever time you want
to paint that particular tree in an autumn landscape, then you
have some idea of the reasons for making a study.

After you have accumulated a considerable number of accurately made studies, you will have enough material to compose
many a studio picture without the need of ever going outdoors.
But you will still need inspiration, or a central idea, for each of
your pictures, and you may have to make a journey outside to
find it.

The study is most important for the professional artist who

must make his livelihood out of his paintings. I have no doubt that the professional artist would prefer to spend more of his time working from nature than indoors. That is where you, painting for pleasure and relaxation, have the advantage.

FOURTEEN

How to Paint Sunlight

ANYONE WHO has not always lived in a desert country knows that the sun does not shine all the time, yet the effort of most beginners is to paint sunlight, and the desire of most of the public is to see pictures with plenty of sunlight in them. It is for the very advanced painter and the cultivated public to enjoy landscapes when nature is not in her sunny moods.

Well, as one who has had considerable experience in what is known as "market research," if sunshine is what people want, let's give them sunshine.

It may just be that I have been lucky in being able to depict sunshine in many of my pictures. Many Week-end Painters have asked me how I do it. This has forced me to study my own techniques with as much objectivity as I can summon. The main thing, as I see it, is to paint a sunny scene just as it appears to be. What is probably the dominating influence in my method of painting sunlight is the discovery I made a few years back that I had been playing all my "tunes" on only two or three octaves of a ten-octave keyboard. Without the consequent conscious effort on my part to utilize the highest and lowest Values of colors, I doubt if anything that I ever painted from a sunny motive would have appeared very sunny.

Only by striving to utilize both the highest and lowest Values whenever they appeared in my subject has it been possible for me to achieve control and put an acceptable simulation of sunshine into my pictures. Whether this suggestion is or is not sound I do not know, but it is my opinion that, until one learns by practice to use both the highest and lowest Values and to acquire that unrestricted freedom of action, the absence of which limits most beginners to Values between 4 and 7, any attempts to depict sunshine will be disappointing. I believe this because the variations of Values in a sunny scene, from the lightest to the darkest, are greatest when the sun is brightest and least on a cloudy day.

Production of a "sunlit" canvas involves more than painting in a "higher key," as some artists and critics put it; or, to borrow a musical simile, it is more than a transposition of one musical key to a higher pitch. Nevertheless, such a Value transposition will aid in giving the lighter or higher Values to the lighter parts of the picture. The weakness of the principle of transposition upward lies in the fact that the darker portions are also raised in Value when, actually, they should be lowered. Thus putting sunlight into a picture seems to me to involve an exaggeration of contrasts—an expansion of the deviation of Values from the median of 5. Of course, there is much more to it than this simple mechanistic concept, but this seems to be the fundamental basis on which the whole procedure of painting sunlight rests.

Arthur S. Allen, who made a huge number of measurements of the color—Hue, Value, and Chroma—in the works of many artists, both living and dead, once told me that most pictures will average 5 Value when analyzed by his methods. Some few artists—a very few—habitually paint in a higher key and will average 6 Value. But to paint a 6-value or a 7-value picture is merely to paint a very light picture; it does not mean that the picture will impress the beholder as one in which sunlight is present. An accurately painted picture of a shore scene where the sky was clouded but where the beach was white sand or crushed oyster shells conceivably might turn out to be a 6-value picture, but it would have no sunlight in it.

Painting sunlight into a picture is not "giving it a bath of sunlight," as I once read in a novel. A charlatan had persuaded

the owner of some fine pictures that they needed his ministra-
tions (at a very handsome fee, as I recall the yarn). The so-
called "bath of sunlight" may have been a thin wash of Gamboge, but that is not the way to get sunlight. The proper procedure, if you are to produce a satisfying result, is not one of
superficial but one of fundamental treatment. Aside from the
method of exaggerating the Value deviations from the median,
the handling of the high lights is important to produce the desired illusion.

Careful study of a subject illuminated by brilliant sunlight
will reveal many places where the Values are so high that they
appear to be pure white. This may require much study on your
part, for there seems to be an optical trick involved. In Chap.
XII, "Painting the Picture," it was pointed out that very small
areas of color appear merely as dark spots. In high lights something of the same thing seems to be involved, only in reverse. A
high light on the arm of my bright red leather chair is really
white or can be painted as white, but the person who sees the
actual object never for one moment thinks that there is a white
spot on the leather, despite the whiteness of the high light. Our
eyes fool us at some times and do not fool us at others. This
time they do not fool us. We still see the red leather chair, not a
chair with a white blemish on it.

The point is that a judicious use of white paint in small areas
of high light in sunlight helps to stimulate the unconscious imagination of the beholder. His impression is that the color of
the immediately adjacent areas is the same as the higher Value
white which is between them.

Backgrounds in intense sunlight are generally of higher Value
and of weaker Chroma than are backgrounds on gray days.
Foregrounds, to the contrary, are only slightly higher in Value
but are much stronger in Chroma. To achieve the proper foreground effects I have often found it necessary to paint the fore-

ground in an irregular mosaic manner in order to utilize optical blending of the colors and to avoid the darkening effect of physical blending of the pigments. There is, however, this precaution to be observed: you must be sure that each and every color of your irregular mosaic is of the proper Value, for if they are different Values the result is very bad. The eye does not blend different Values as well as it does different Chromas and not nearly so well as it does different Hues of the same Value and Chroma.

These few suggestions may help you as you experiment in portraying sunlight. Though there appears to be a definite scientific principle involved—the expansion of the deviation of Values from the median—there is no easy mechanical way to do a sunlit picture.

Plates VI and VII show how I painted the same scene at widely separated intervals. The first was done in my "4-to-7-value" days. The second was done much later. It depicts sunlight by spreading the Values.

FIFTEEN

How to Paint a Tree

IN LANDSCAPE painting there is no element of composition more frequently used than a tree. Although trees are very common and most of us see them every day, they are, like everything else that appears commonplace, difficult to paint well. Probably the most difficult thing to paint well is the human face, while skies, waves, and trees are almost as difficult.

After reading everything on tree painting I have been able to lay my hands on and studying the techniques of good artists whose pictures can be seen in exhibitions and galleries, I have evolved my own method of tree painting. It never occurred to me that my ideas would be of any benefit to others until an elderly chap one day stopped his car near my easel and asked permission to watch me work. This I willingly granted but with the admonition that he not stand directly behind me, for I always wear a path back from my easel and might step on him inadvertently. Soon I forgot that he was there. Perhaps thirty minutes later he exclaimed, "So that's how to paint a tree?"

"Well, it's my way to paint a tree."

"I am greatly indebted to you, sir. I have been trying to teach myself to do a tree for a year, and so far I have made no progress."

At other times I have been asked about tree painting and have tried to aid other struggling self-taught artists with the little that I have been able to dig up for myself. Though I am far from satisfied with my own trees, I shall try to describe here how I go about them. Perhaps you can improve on my methods.

A little tree on a small canvas can be suggested with a single brush stroke. That sort of tree is not much of a problem. But a tree that is to occupy a space from 3 to 12 inches high on your canvas requires some real painting. Analysis of a tree will show the need to grasp its structural characteristics, its method of branching, the stiffness or droop of the smaller limbs. I was never able to do a reasonably good tree until I learned all about what botanists call the "habits of growth." If I am doing an elm tree, I want it to look like an elm, not like a maple. In the winter you can identify most of the common species of trees without the aid of the leaves, even though you are not a botanist. The structure of the trunk and branches is enough for identification.

With this in mind, I begin by painting the trunk and branches of the whole tree before I put on the foliage. In other words, I now paint a tree in much the same manner that I have been told is occasionally used by fashion artists who draw the nude human figure and then put the clothes on it. I have heard that some even draw the skeleton, then put on the flesh, and then the clothes.

In summer, with the tree in full leaf, it is not always easy to see just where the limbs are, but you can always walk around the tree and look upward from underneath to discover how it is built. After doing this, I begin to draw it on my canvas as accurately as I can, taking great care that all measurements are checked and double checked. Usually I draw with a pencil and have a gum eraser handy to make corrections. The principal problem is to get the total height of the tree in proper relation to the overall width of the foliage. The next problem is to draw the visible part of the trunk in proper relationship to the branches and to have the diameter correct in relation to the weight it must bear. Some folks make their trunks too spindly; some too thick. The oak is the principal tree that has a trunk which is thick in proportion to its height or overall diameter.

With these limits accurately fixed, the drawing in of the main branches is simple if done with care (see Fig. 19, between pages 92 and 93. If you are careless, though, you may discover that the tree is growing larger than you had planned it in your composition. When this occurs there is nothing to do but erase and start over. (Too much erasure, however, may remove the sizing from the canvas.)

The principal large branches are drawn first, whether they are visible through the foliage or not. I do not recommend drawing them all in great detail because oil paint is opaque and will cover up many of the smaller lines as soon as you start painting. But I definitely counsel that whatever you draw be done with all the accuracy you can command.

At this stage you should have on your canvas a drawing of the trunk and of the main branches of the tree (see Fig. 19). The angles of the branches from the trunk must be exactly right, for this is one of the characteristics of the various kinds of trees. Certain pines have branches that stick out at right angles to the trunk. Apple trees never branch from the trunk in this manner, but many of the secondary branches are at right angles to the main branches. The American elm has an acute angle between branches and trunk, narrower than the corresponding angle of a maple. And so on.

I repeat: never be careless about the drawing of the tree structure, for this is the foundation on which the foliage must be put. If it is not correctly drawn, the ensuing work will be handicapped, if not ruined. It is easy to fall into the bad habit of suggestion by a crudely—nay carelessly—drawn line where the branch is to go. I have seen some attempts that looked like the top ends of feather dusters, and, needless to say, the resultant tree pictures lacked any resemblance to their subjects. You may promise yourself that, though the pencil line is carelessly drawn, when you come to painting in the branch you will do it with consummate care and skill. But, like most of our promises to ourselves, this one is too easily broken.

I have seldom seen a painting that was started carelessly which ended well. It is better to exert yourself to the utmost from the beginning. We all have had the sad experience of starting out bravely with a fresh canvas and ending up a long way from our expectations. Get the tree drawing right before doing anything more. (This admonition applies to every other part of the picture as well.)

Having accurately completed the drawing of the tree and all the other parts of the picture, it is now time to start painting. Here I shall describe only the painting of the tree itself. My own first move is usually to paint in the sky holes, for I find it much easier to paint the tree over the sky than to put sky into the holes of the foliage. Some painters, however, prefer the opposite method. Sky holes are generally slightly darker and grayer than the large areas of sky visible above and beside the tree; you will probably discover this for yourself after you have painted your first twenty-five trees.

It is not desirable to paint in the whole sky behind the tree, for if you do you will have to lay wet paint onto wet paint, which is a tough job for a beginner. Put in just enough sky to cover the small spots where the sky shows through. The rest of the canvas to be covered by the tree should be left bare at this stage.

The second step is to put in the trunk and branches with the utmost skill that you can employ. Even though you expect to cover many of the branches with foliage, do not slight them in any way. You can see enough of the visible branches to decide what Hue they have, what Value, and what Chroma. Branches that are away from you will be grayer, that is, more neutral in color than those which are close. Those which are on the shady side of the tree will be darker than those on the sunny side. The undersides will be darker than the tops. The lower branches will be more nearly on a level with your eye than those which are higher up; hence the lower and generally shady side of the upper branches will be visible (where you can see them through openings in the foliage).

When the painting has reached this stage the skeleton of the tree should appear much as it does when the leaves are all off (see Fig. 19). There is, however, one important difference. The leaves of a large tree weigh probably a ton or more. With all this weight, the branches of a tree in full leaf will droop considerably lower than one without any leaves. I learned this to my dismay one autumn in Vermont when I had been working on an autumn landscape for four successive mornings. I was just about ready to put on the glorious autumn foliage when a strong gust of wind tore off almost every leaf from the biggest tree in the landscape. It blew over my easel as well, but that was a much less serious problem than the disappearance of the foliage and, still more important, the greatly stiffened appearance of the tree. Relieved of the immense weight of the foliage, the branches assumed a more vertical position—so much so that for a moment I was puzzled to explain how I could possibly have made such a grievous error in my drawing. Fortunately I had taken some 5-by-7 photographs the day before, being fearful that a rain might prevent my finishing the painting before I should have to go home from my little holiday. Later, by comparing my drawing of the branches with the photographs, I was able to prove to myself that I had made no error, that the changed angles were a result of the removal of the great weight of leaves that had bent the branches downward.

Now comes the painting in of the foliage. To make the discussion as simple as possible, let us assume that this is a tree in summer with all the foliage in one general color—green. At this stage, you should study carefully its various Hues, Values, and Chromas. The actual painting of the foliage can be done very

Plates VI and VII. PUTTING SUNLIGHT INTO A PICTURE

The sunlight effect is obtained by expanding the deviation of the
Values from the mean. of 5 Value. In the gray picture the highest
Value is 8, and the lowest is 4. When the same subject was re-
painted in the studio, the deviation of the Values was expanded so
that the highest Value is now about 9½ and the lowest is 2. Many
persons prefer the gray picture to the one depicting glaring sunlight,
but if you want to introduce sunlight this is the way to do it.

rapidly if the color analysis has been made correctly and ample quantities of the proper paints have been mixed and are ready for use.

Some artists will mix a little dab of color and apply it, then mix another little dab and apply that, and so on ad infinitum— or at least until the picture has been filled in. Sometimes a picture can be done well by this method, but usually a beginner will have trouble making successive batches of color look as if they were all made to match the foliage of a single tree. Usually I mix four or five batches of different Values at once, some of them as large as walnuts or even larger if the tree is a large one.

On the side of the tree nearest the artist there will be three or more Values, roughly speaking, the lightest being nearest the source of light—the sun—the darkest being on the shady side, with the middle Values being probably nearest to the beholder. One way of painting the foliage is to mix a green that is as close a match as possible to the middle Value of the near side of the tree. Then divide this mixture into three parts, lighten one with white paint for the sunny side, and darken the other with Payne's Gray, black, or a black mixture of red, yellow, and blue; or, if you are very "persnickity," you can make a dark green by the addition of a greater proportion of red and blue to your yellow, provided you are sufficiently adept at mixing to be certain that you have the same green. You will now have, I hope, enough of the three colors to paint the near side of the tree, but it is not yet time to apply them. There are still more colors to mix—those for the parts of the tree that are farther away from the eye, whether they can be seen from below or through holes in the foliage at the front.

These greens will, of course, be all of the same original basis, for a healthy tree has the same sort of foliage on all sides, but the greens of the farther side will have a somewhat weaker Chroma and different Values from the greens that are nearest to the eye. Ordinarily there will be very little of the back side of the tree visible from the front; but, unless that little is done properly, your tree will have a strange appearance. In fact, it may even look as if the whole back of the tree had been left off or as if a giant knife had descended from heaven and sliced it away.

When mixing the weaker Chroma paint for the back of the tree, it is advisable to keep in mind the principle of exaggeration, or accentuation, and neutralize the greens slightly in order to produce the illusion of depth from front to back. Some writer has said that a well-painted tree is one into which and through which a bird could fly. If this impression is not created, the tree will appear to be too solid and will have a puffball effect that is hard to eliminate.

Just how much color and how many different kinds of color to mix in advance can only be learned from judgment and experience. But it is better to be on the generous side. If all is in readiness and plenty of clean paintbrushes are laid out, you are now prepared to begin painting in the foliage.

I must digress here on the matter of suitable brushes. There is no set rule about which brush to use that I have ever heard of —or any sort of brush that gives the best results so far as my experience goes. Paint can be applied with a palette knife as well as with a brush. When using brushes, the choice depends on the sort of brushwork you desire to employ. And there are many types of brushwork, as you can readily observe by going to any gallery or exhibition.

One way to apply paint for tree foliage that I have found very effective is to use a round brush and almost to *roll* the paint on the canvas from the side of the brush (see Fig. 19). Notice that I said "roll" it on rather than "brush" it on. The brush needs to be round rather than flat, for a flat brush will not roll effectively if it is more than ¼ inch wide. After I had got the hang of the rolling method I used nothing else for a long time, but in recent years I have also adopted other methods. The rolling method is satisfactory for producing drooping foliage, but if the foliage is of a different type, held by stiff branches, then rolling will not be suitable.

A stiff, flat brush, used to brush the paint on from its tip, will produce a very different type of foliage. And wide brushes will produce effects different from narrow brushes; likewise long strokes will produce different effects than short strokes. Great variety can be obtained by different ways of handling and holding the brush. Experience gained from many attempts to paint trees will show you how to produce in your paintings the foliage that you see. The best advice I can give you is to experiment, but when you are trying different ways of brushing be sure that they are really different. Watch out for a habitual method which, should it unhappily fail to produce the desired results, might be difficult for you to correct.

Another method of painting a tree is what might be termed the "sandwich method." Here the back of the tree is painted first. Then the branches are painted onto the wet backside. Next the near side is laid onto the branches. However, I have not found this method very satisfactory in my own work.

~~~~~~

SIXTEEN

"Clean" Color

SOME ARTISTS can paint a picture with a clarity of color or a sense of "cleanness" as refreshing as a cool breeze on a stuffy day. Others habitually produce pictures in colors to which no other terms than "muddy" or "dirty" can be applied. They do this even when using oil paints, which are more difficult to muddy than water colors.

"Dirty" colors are just what their name implies. A picture done in dirty colors will, at its most aggravated, look almost as if someone had shaken a dust mop over the wet canvas; yet extraneous dirt has nothing whatever to do with the effect.

Clean colors have a limpid freshness that is most satisfying. If you fail to produce a picture that has the characteristic of clean color, the fault is your own. You can be certain of this because all paints as squeezed from the tube are "fresh" or "clean" in appearance. Something that you do produces the muddy, or dirty, appearance.

What is the cause of dirty color? How is it defined?

In all my readings and conversations I do not recall ever having learned the answer to these foregoing questions, so what I shall say about dirty color is the result of my own investigations.

Dirty color seems to me to be the result of nothing more than, first, bits of low-value (darker) colors showing up as specks or streaks in the midst of higher Value (lighter) colors or, second, low-value (dark) colors showing up through *opaque* high-value (light) colors. I emphasize "opaque" because someone may think I am neglecting the technique known as "glazing." As a matter of fact, glazing is really the reverse procedure of painting over a dry, high-value (light) color with a thin, *transparent*, low-value (dark) color in order to obtain the effect of optical—in contrast to physical—blending. If, however, a dark color underneath shows up through a thin coat of *opaque* paint that is lighter, or has a higher Value than itself, the effect is not optical blending but mostly muddiness.

Let us consider the first type of muddiness or dirty color. One procedure in mixing colors on the palette starts by mixing the necessary colors to produce the Hue desired, then adds the complementary colors to reduce the Chroma to the desired intensity, and lastly adds white to lighten the mixture to the desired Value. This routine on my own palette invariably produces a clean color (not to be confused with a chalky one, produced by too much white and/or turpentine), but deviation from the sequence sometimes produces dirty color.

A simple experiment will show you one of several causes of dirty color. Mix a little very light blue paint of about 8 or 9 Value. Then mix in a little raw umber. Don't mix the two too much. Spread the color out on a clean place on your palette, and observe the brown streaks that give it a muddy effect. Next mix it thoroughly, and see the streaks and the muddiness disappear. Incomplete mixing of low- and very high-value colors is one cause of muddiness.

But the foregoing suggestion is not to be construed as a blanket endorsement of complete mixing—far from it. Incomplete mixing is one of the methods of securing vibrancy of color, as explained in Chap. VI. The masters of this technique were the Impressionists—Monet, Pissarro, Sisley, Childe Hassam, and so forth—yet if you study their paintings you will find that they never mixed colors incompletely where high- and low-value colors were juxtaposed. You will see that they used colors of nearly equal Value for incomplete mixing and that their effects are generally pleasing. My own experiments indicate that the effects become more pleasing the closer the Values of the compoents of the mixture are to each other.

A variant of this source of dirty color, arising from the same general cause, occurs when you accidentally mix high and low Values on the canvas itself when you attempt to put fresh paint over wet paint. It really is quite a trick to apply color over wet paint and avoid mixing the two layers. The trick is doubly difficult for the beginner, whose previous experience with a paintbrush has consisted of painting floors or woodwork and who therefore considers brushing out to a smooth coat to be a virtue. When painting a picture on canvas never employ the brushwork of a house painter. Rather, put the color on, and leave it alone even if it lies there in gobs.

Putting a high-value paint over a wet, low-value paint can be done, however, without the undesired mixing and without bringing up bits of the darker paint to the surface. But it takes lots of practice to do well, especially when a bristle brush is used. If the brush has any frayed or curled bristles that stick out instead of lying flat, they will almost surely contribute to the undesirable mixing. The remedy is to trim off the offending bristles with scissors or else use a new brush—at least use a good one. Another way to paint over wet paint is to use a Russian-sable brush, the hairs of which are so soft that they cannot dig up any of the soft underpaint. This is about the only use I have ever found for costly Russian-sable oil brushes. A third way to avoid the unwanted mixing of top and bottom colors is to apply the top paint with a palette knife.

The palette knife is used in painting in order to "trowel on" the paint. It is far less likely to produce undesired mixing on the canvas than a bristle brush. But even a palette knife has its limitations, and one who messes, fusses, and niggles can produce muddy effects with anything if he keeps at it long enough. Perseverance will produce results, even in spoiling a picture.

Another way to avoid the undesired mixing of light and dark paints on the canvas is simply to scrape off the unwanted paint before applying any other color. You can scrape it off either with your palette knife or with a grapefruit knife, right down to the dry surface. Then start painting again.

There are still other causes of dirty paint, such as the use of black to darken a high-value (light) color. Black has its purposes, but one of them is not to darken a very light paint, especially one of low Chroma. Another cause of muddiness in colors that I have observed, though fortunately I have never experienced it myself, seems to be associated with putting Cadmium Red into a mixture where it should never be used in the first place. Cadmium Red is useful only when you need an exceptionally high-chroma scarlet.

We come now to the second type of muddy color, where the dark color underneath shows through the opaque light color on top. This occurs most frequently for me when I am trying to paint a very light opaque color over a dark color that has already dried. If the upper paint is applied too thinly, the lower one will show through and not often be pleasing. The remedy is simple: put on more paint, or put on two or three coats.

After you have been painting for a long time, say five or ten years, you will overcome the problem of muddy color without any advice or instruction provided you seek its causes. But until you learn the causes and their remedies, you will be very like the beginner learning to drive a car and repeatedly killing his engine. An experienced driver finds it is almost impossible to kill his engine.

The causes of muddy color have their origin chiefly in an artist's psychological approach to his work. If you have enough self-control to put your colors onto the canvas and not work over and over them, you will have cleaner paint than if you insist on monkeying around. But, of course, this presupposes that you have put on the correct colors in the first place.

The next time you read in your newspaper about an exhibition of paintings and the critic refers to someone's "fresh colors," you will know that it is his way of saying that the artist has avoided some of the problems that have been enumerated here. Anybody who is not color blind can identify muddy colors, but few, indeed, know their causes or how to overcome them.

~~~~~~

SEVENTEEN

Critics and Criticism

A CHAP IN Pennsylvania once showed me one of his paintings, asking, "Please tell me how I could make this a better picture." That is the right spirit for anyone who is really seeking to improve his work.

How different, however, was another incident that happened many years ago when I was in college. Two students from the art department had allowed me to go along when they went out on a sketching trip one Saturday. After both had worked for a while, the first stood his panel up against a tree and called to the other, "I say, old man, give me a criticism."

The other chap, a bit of a harum-scarum, stood his picture against another tree and complied. What he had to say about the first picture would properly be termed "blistering." The first student flew into a violent rage, rushed over to the critic's picture, and kicked a hole in it. The ensuing brawl was one of the most entertaining I have ever witnessed. I tell of it to show the wrong way to criticize and the wrong manner in which to receive criticism.

Criticism from one who knows his stuff is very helpful, for in theory, at least, the critic is showing you what is wrong with your work and how to make it better. But competent criticism is often difficult to get. I have known amateurs who paid $5 to a professional for a fifteen-minute criticism—not a lesson in painting, merely a criticism. Usually a good painter is too fed up with amateurish attempts to paint to want to give a beginner careful criticism without compensation unless he happens to be his close personal friend. The professional painters with whom

I go out sketching never volunteer any comments on my work. Sometimes professionals actually shy away from being drawn into criticizing. Criticism is a real job, requiring study and concentration, to say nothing of the possibility that the one whose work is criticized may react most unhappily. If you pay for criticism, it is to be expected that you really want to know the truth; then the critic knows that he is free to tell you what he really feels.

Critics who do not know how to paint are of little help to the beginner, for they are generally very vague about what they imagine to be wrong; or they may think that their duty is to express appreciative or complimentary remarks about something that is no good; or, as is more often the case, they are concerned only with the subject matter of the picture rather than with techniques.

The layman who knows nothing about painting, however, can sometimes tell what is wrong with a picture or even point out something that is wrong in a certain area without being able to say exactly what it is. Often such criticism is helpful, although the ideal form of criticism is accurate and competent information about what is wrong, why it is wrong, and how to correct it.

When a critic merely says, "I don't like this part," or, "I'd like to see a little more feeling here," or makes similar generalities, I for one cannot get much benefit from his remarks. Immediately I want to know what the critic dislikes or *how* I am to put in more "feeling" or what is "feeling," anyway? This is not to decry the effort of the critic but to point out that such criticism is not competent, is not helpful, or is overpoetic and probably only suited to the advanced student.

But when the critic says something like the following, the beginner may derive much benefit from his criticism: "Your tree is solid, like a puffball. It lacks open air in the spaces between the leaves. I would suggest painting it over after scraping off the wet paint. Study the tree colors, and observe that there are several colors in the foliage. Mix up a gob of each color. Be sure that the colors in the shadow, especially those at the back of the tree, are properly neutralized to get the effect of distance from front to back. In fact, I would counsel overneutralizing them. Also it would be helpful if you would exaggerate the differences between the high lights and the low lights. When you begin to paint, work from back to front. Paint in your sky holes first, being sure that the sky is sufficiently neutralized so that it is very *far* back of the tree instead of so close that the foliage appears to be imbedded in the sky."

Here is another helpful type of criticism:

"Your barn looks too new and up-to-date to be interesting. You have not captured the charm of age. Your colors are right, but your drawing is wrong. You have unconsciously repaired all the ravages of time. Your roof line is straight, as if the barn had just been built, but the ridge has sunk several inches through the years. The roof is really swaybacked. No matter whether you have drawn it as you see it, if you want to make it an *old* barn you must accentuate the things that tell the story of its age. You must exaggerate the depression in the ridge line in order to make your picture show what you have seen and felt."

Or the following:

"Your picture is flat. It lacks depth. Everything is in the same plane. I do not feel that I am able to go back into the picture without running smack up against a solid surface. To correct this defect, you must emphasize the differences of Chroma between front and back. If you will overneutralize the colors in the background and increase the Chroma of the colors in the foreground, you will discover that depth will begin to come into your picture. The only two ways in which we can produce the illusion of a third dimension are by linear perspective and color perspective. You have utilized the former, but you have not employed the latter effectively. No, I don't recommend starting all over again unless you really would feel happier doing so. I would make the corrections right on the wet canvas."

Comments like these are real instruction, and the recipient should be most gratified that someone who knows more about art than he does has taken the time to help him.

If somebody doesn't like what I have painted, that is his prerogative. If he doesn't like it and tells me so, I immediately want to know what it is he doesn't like, why, and what to do about it.

You should be prepared for the know-it-all who looks wise and makes cynical comments merely to produce the impression on others that he is very, very intelligent. What he says means nothing. Usually he is not honest enough to tell you that he does not know much about art and cannot say why he doesn't like your work.

In painting a picture the beginner often has an experience that is exactly parallel to that of the novice writing a story. The writer has a story in mind. It is very vivid in his imagination. It excites him, and when he speaks of it to others it excites them. Therefore, it must be a good story. He will write it and sell it to a magazine. But when it is sent out to the magazine it is promptly returned with the usual printed rejection slip. Not often is he able to get the competent criticism that will tell him why it is no good. He may accumulate as many as twenty rejection slips before he concludes that the story is really worthless. Frequently, the only difficulty is that he has not put down on paper the same story that he had in mind. Experiencing a good story is common to all humanity, but the ability to impart all the effects of the experience to others—that takes skill and experience.

In the same way the artist is confronted with an identical problem. He must translate his own emotional experiences onto the canvas. If he has the technique to do this at his command he is more likely to portray his ideas successfully than the artist who has not. But there are times when artists are more successful in imparting their own emotions than they are in painting well, just as an illiterate person who maltreats the English language may yet be able to tell a fascinating tale that holds one's attention for hours. Such artistic "illiteracy" often gives rise to vast controversies over the merits and demerits of the artist's work. Take some of Paul Cézanne's paintings, for instance, or Vincent van Gogh's. If you ever try to copy a Van Gogh, you will discover that he was a very careless worker. He has shadows going in various directions or no shadows at all where shadows should be, and often his brushwork is of the sloppiest character imaginable; but no one can successfully deny that Van Gogh was a great painter. His works are great because of the very intensity of the feeling he was able to impart to his canvas, which in turn arouses a comparable feeling in the beholder. He was great in spite of his minor defects—things that lesser artists would never be guilty of. Yet how few could ever achieve one-tenth of 1 per cent of the genius of Van Gogh!

Paul Cézanne experienced great emotions which he succeeded in conveying to canvas despite his reiterated complaint that he never could "realize" (on canvas) what he felt. Many of Cézanne's pictures are very poor from the technical viewpoint. I should hate to think I was condemned to do as poor a technical job as he often did, but what he had to say and the intensity of the manner in which he said it have made Cézanne one of the great artists of all time.

Ability to spell correctly, to write grammatically, and to organize literary material into a logical story or essay cannot make a great writer. Nor can ability to paint with technical perfection make a great artist.

Much of the controversy about Modernism in art arises from

differences of opinion as to what is good painting. There seem to me to be two types of Modernists: those who can't paint, and those who can but won't. By this I mean that some Moderns are really great painters, having superb technical ability, such as Salvador Dali. (Boy! can that fellow paint!) But for some reason they choose to paint subject matter that I would not hang in my home. Then there are others who are imitators and mistake the form for the substance, and hence I say they cannot paint.

Once I saw a well-known professional whose paintings I much admire gazing intently at a very messy Modern painting. As he was turning away, I said to him, "I should like to get your opinion of Modernism in art."

For a time he refused to speak his mind, but after further questioning he finally opened up. "Painting," said he, "is both a trade and a profession. A good painter is master of both. To master the trade—the craftsmanship of good painting—requires many years of constant effort. Some artists who profess to be Moderns, by the very character of their work, are masters of the trade. They know how to paint well, and, if they choose to affect their queer perspectives and strange grotesqueries or if they are more interested in the morbid than the beautiful, I have no quarrel with them. They paint what they like to paint, even as I. But there are many others who do not know their trade, do not know how to do their Modernistic pictures with skill, are so lacking in understanding that they see only what appears to be haphazard daubs. I can see and understand what the first type are doing, though I would never admire it, but the second type, who have never learned their trade, are giving Modernism a worse reputation than it deserves."

People who have little sales resistance will accept criticisms more easily than those rugged individualists who insist on doing

things in their own way. The former are apt to be too strongly
influenced by the ideas of the critic, whereas the latter will probably benefit less than they should. While I am not sympathetic
to a man who, like Adrian Hill (in his book *On Painting Trees*),
refuses to say very much lest the student learn to paint the way
he paints, I am not at all sold on the sort of teaching that makes
a student paint exactly like his teacher. To illustrate: usually
you can spot the work of a student of Anthony Thieme, of
Rockport, Massachusetts, or a pupil of the late William
Bruestle, of Old Lyme, Connecticut, or one of Eliot O'Hara,
of Goose Rocks, Maine. You can spot it because so often it
looks as if the master himself had done it. I like the work of
these men, but, when I go to an exhibit of their pupils and
find that nearly all the canvases appear to have been done by
the same person in a manner that is almost a duplicate of the
master's style, then I believe there has been too much ac-
ceptance of teaching and criticism and not enough independ-
ence on the part of the student. When a student succumbs so
completely to the overpowering personality of a teacher, it is
time for him to change teachers. Which is not to disparage
the teacher.

I have discovered when week-end painting that my own
comments on a fellow painter's work can influence him to
paint in the manner I suggest. On one man this influence was so
marked that at the time our wives were not sure whose canvases
were which. This was admittedly an extreme case—a case of
overvigorous suggestion. There is a happy medium between
not enough and too much.

There is also the type of critic who fairly exudes "culture"
and who frequently speaks on art but cannot answer a sensible
technical question. Such a person once gave a lecture on art in
my town and spoke glowingly of the "rich colors" of some of
the Old Masters, especially some of the Pre-Raphaelites. When

the talk was over I asked the speaker to tell me what was *rich* color. This brought forth a five-minute torrent of words that meant exactly nothing. I repeated my question: "What is rich color? If I wanted to do a painting in rich color, what should I use?" The speaker turned from me in disgust, remarking, "Oh, you're a scientist!" as if I had been rude and uncouth. The plain fact is that she did not know what rich color was. Such critics may be all right for the dilletantes, but give me a meatier diet, please.

"Criticism," as a word, has acquired a meaning that it never should have. As commonly used, "to criticize" means "to condemn" or "to speak adversely" about the thing or action criticized.

If you are asked to "criticize" a picture, it should not mean that you find every possible fault with it or disparage the work of the artist. Rather, criticism is a careful examination done in a critical vein with the intention of finding the good elements as well as the bad. Art criticism should be constructive, if possible, and of course that implies the services of a competent critic—one who knows his stuff.

To be of maximum value, criticism should be given with the idea of aiding the artist to make his work better. If you can't bear criticism or if it makes you smart from injured feelings, you should learn to develop a thicker skin.

EIGHTEEN

Brief Observations on Painting

NEVER PAINT in the shade of a small catalpa or sycamore tree when the sun is shining brightly. The large leaves are translucent, and beneath them your canvas will be bathed in a yellow-green light that will confuse your color selection. Usually it will cause you to paint a very unsatisfactory sketch.

❋　❋

If you visit galleries, you will observe that most worth-while paintings are on fairly large canvases. While some of the world's great pictures, of course, are very small, the majority are larger than 20 by 24 inches. This suggests the desirability of doing a fairly large picture yourself now and then, after you have progressed to the point where you feel like doing something larger than the usual 12-by-16 panel.

❋　❋

In the Boston Museum of Art there is an unfinished landscape by Paul Cézanne that merits study if you ever have the opportunity. It is painted on a very fine-textured buff canvas. In particular, it shows how Cézanne started a picture. When he painted a sky, he omitted all paint from the areas that were obviously intended for clouds. To me the important feature is that his brush strokes did *not* outline the clouds; apparently his brushes were pushed, bristles foremost, toward the cloud areas and then lifted. This left an irregular soft edge.

❋　❋

All good artists seem to write a superb hand, which bespeaks
well-trained muscles. It is not necessary for all your exercise
to be gained wielding a brush or pencil.

Hand and wrist exercises are excellent if you find that your
free-hand drawing is poor. Describing large figure eights both
forward and backward with the fingers extended is also helpful.

❋ ❋

How much light should you allow on your canvas while painting? Too little is as bad as too much. I once measured the
illumination *reflected* from a fresh canvas in the studio of a
famous artist, Percival Rosseau. It was 2 foot-candles. The
direct reading of the north sky light coming through the studio
windows was 62 foot-candles. Corresponding readings in the
studio of Richard Marintreu in London were ½ and 30 foot-
candles.

❋ ❋

Artificial illumination can be used for painting, provided
you correct for the color deficiencies. If ordinary incandescent
lamps are used, the light will be predominantly red and yellow
and will be deficient in blue as compared to daylight from a
north sky. This deficiency can be corrected by burning a blue
lamp or a "daylight" (slightly blue) lamp in addition to so-
called "white" bulbs. The ideal lamp, however, is the fluo-
rescent.

❋ ❋

Where I live, I am frequently troubled by the red reflection
from a neighboring brick wall when the sun strikes full on it. I
am able to correct this somewhat by burning a blue lamp in
my studio.

❋ ❋

Reflected light from green trees outside bothered one artist so much that he cut down all the trees for 300 feet north of his studio.

* *

If you paint at home you need not fear spoiling your rugs by dropping paint on them unless you are an exceptionally careless and messy person. On my own studio floor there is a fine Chinese rug, and only twice have I ever dropped paint on it. This was quickly removed by scraping it up with a clean palette knife, then rubbing the spot with a *clean* turkish towel, wiping it clean with a cloth dampened by turpentine, and, finally, wiping it dry with a clean towel.

* *

Some artists seem to need several extra pairs of hands to hold their brushes when painting. I have actually seen a woman artist holding six brushes and a palette in her left hand and two more brushes in her mouth like a gigantic moustache.

* *

After you have painted for a few years you will be astonished at the deviations made by other artists—even famous artists— from what you consider to be the proper relation between the Values of sky and earth. Some good artists habitually paint very dark skies even in what are supposed to be sunny scenes.

* *

Value (light and dark) is more important than color.

It's a good thing to paint in monochrome now and then, especially if you can't make your objects stand out on the canvas. Monochrome, as the name implies, is a single color. Burnt Umber is a better monochrome than Lampblack or

Ivory Black because it has a higher Chroma and is more satisfying to use. Use only the one color and white.

Monochrome forces you to develop your chiaroscuro—your
use of light and dark. All ordinary photography is in monochrome. What the camera can do, you can do—sometimes to
better effect!

When painting in monochrome, always use a very low-value
color, or you cannot properly render your darks.

❊   ❊

It's quite a trick for a beginner to determine if his Values
are correct because there are so many different colors in his
picture. One way to do it is to study the reflections of the picture in a black mirror. It is said that this sort of mirror reflects
only lights and darks, not Hues, thereby enabling the artist
to judge his Values.

Since I have never been able to find a black mirror, I have
had to develop another method. Occasionally I use a Wratten
photographic filter that permits the passage of only a single
color—red (Wratten A No. 25). By viewing my picture
through this red filter I can see it in monochrome. This means
that everything is in one color and enables me to discover
whether my lights and darks are properly done. To be sure,
this is only a trick, or device, for self-criticism that has on rare
occasions been of slight use to me.

To my way of thinking, a better system is to contemplate the
subject and register in your own mind how light or how dark
are the Hues observed. Then try to match the Values in paint,
and put them on the canvas.

❊   ❊

It's a good plan to stop now and then and clean up your
palette, particularly if things are going badly. Many a time it
will seem to be well nigh impossible to mix the right color;

your palette will be covered with gobs of wrong colors. Right then is a good moment to scrape everything off but your tube colors, take a fresh smoke, and walk around a bit. Then start afresh. Sometimes a lot of daubs of the wrong colors will be so discouraging that a fresh start like this is the best way to conserve your time.

* *

Once I was painting on a dock in the Hudson River when a chap with his little daughter asked permission to watch. After a half hour he said, "Watching you makes me want to get out my old paintbox and go to work."

"Well, why don't you? If you want company, I will be here for at least three more hours."

"No use. I'm color-blind. I went to art school for two years and caught hell about three times a week from my instructors before someone discovered that I was unable to distinguish red from green. Then they told me to give it up."

* *

Don't be "upstage" in your pictures. This is a term borrowed from the theater. In that craft a person who is "upstage" is always far from the audience, at the back of the stage. It is an unattractive form of aloofness, and in the theater it is considered very bad acting. Good actors usually work close to the footlights, except when the business requires them to be elsewhere.

In painting, you should design or construct your pictures so that the center of interest is close—never far away. Being remote in a picture is very much like being upstage in the theater. Remember what Adolph Fassbender said: "The best pictures are the ones close to you, never far away."

If you follow this principle of bringing the subject close to the front of your canvas, you will find that you automatically eliminate a great deal that is superfluous and that contributes little to the idea you are trying to bring out. It will help you simplify your composition.

❊   ❊

Reflections from water are not to be confused with shadows on water, although many people speak as if they were one and the same thing.

Reflections from water gave me no end of trouble until I began to study them with a Weston light meter. Here is what I discovered:

When the sun is at its height (midday) the reflection has about the same Value as the object reflected. But when the sun is away from the zenith there is an increasing divergence between the measurable amount of light reflected by the object to the observer's eye and the amount reflected from the surface of the water to the observer's eye. The divergence is greatest when the sun is near the horizon. At any time up to an hour after sunrise or an hour before sundown the Value of a reflection from water seems to be about one-half the Value of the object reflected.

After learning this, it was a comparatively simple matter for me to paint convincing reflections (see Fig. 21, between pages 92 and 93).

Shadows on water are very different things and do not follow any such general principle. The only rule I know for painting them is careful observation.

❊   ❊

Speaking of reflections: there is a way to paint convincingly the reflections of such things as trees, piles, and the like from deep water with a muddy bottom, a way to get that desired depth or semitransparency of brown-green color. I have found that a very little Prussian Blue or Winsor Blue mixed with a greater amount of Raw Umber or Burnt Umber will give an approximation of the sought-for color. The most important thing is to keep white paint out of the mixture, or it will suddenly lose its semitransparency and become dull and opaque. After you have it on the canvas, you may want to raise the Value a wee bit. But be very cautious about an admixture of white paint. If is often better to raise the Value with Raw Sienna or even Yellow Ochre.

When used in this manner to raise Value, white has the curious property of seeming to be on the surface of water. A few streaks of white drawn across a dark reflection as previously described will usually depict high lights or reflections on the surface.

With these few suggestions you may be able to experiment and produce a satisfactory technique of painting reflections in your own work. If your initial attempts are not satisfactory, do not hesitate to scrape them off and try again. But look out for white. Use it sparingly.

❋   ❋

What seems to me to be one of the more difficult things to paint is a satisfactory blue sky. The problem is to get it to look sufficiently dark blue, yet transparent, with a Chroma that is low enough to make it appear far away.

❋   ❋

Another difficult thing to paint is green grass in the foreground in sunlight. This would not seem to involve any very serious problems, yet it seldom turns out properly, at least to my own critical eye.

Once I was painting at a mountain resort where a professional was giving painting lessons to some youngsters. Later

I asked her about painting grass, and she suggested *underpainting* with purple. Maybe it works for some folks, but it never has for me.

* *

At lunch one day an able illustrator was recounting some of his art-school experiences. I expressed regret that I had never had the opportunity to study art formally. His response may interest you. It was helpful to me.

"If you can *see* color and can mix color and know how to draw, there is little you can gain in a school except lots of practice. Keep on painting. When you get stuck and have no instructor to run to, go to an art gallery, and see how other fellows handled it.

"Furthermore, if you should ever go to an art school, never stay another day after you discover that you are beginning to paint like your instructor. Why? There is no profit for an artist in painting like somebody else. You want to paint in a style that is all your own."

* *

Most commercial artists have what they call "swipe collections." These are collections of clippings, illustrations, drawings, and the like that serve to help them out when something they need is not available. I, too, have my own "swipe collection," which includes among other things photographs of scenes that I should some day like to convert into paintings.

My pictures of figures have been of greatest use to me. Often I have needed a figure to add life to a picture and have had no model from whom to draw. Simple things like a woman sweeping, a man pushing a wheelbarrow or shoveling, or a kid carrying a fish pole are very difficult to find. Once I had to buy a poultry magazine to get a picture of chickens for the barnyard in the frontispiece (Plate I).

A black-and-white reproduction of one of Adolph Fassbender's photographs clipped from a newspaper was the basis
for one of my pictures. He thus supplied the composition and
the Values. All I did was to imagine what the colors ought to be
and put them on. This job (Plate IV) kept me busy for more
than a year on those week ends when I could not work out of
doors directly from nature.

❀　❀

Once you become deeply interested in painting, it will make
very little difference to you whether your Sundays are rainy or
pleasant. There are plenty of pictures to be painted indoors
from older pictures, from your "swipe collection," or from what
you can see out the window.

And then there is still life. One of my painting companions,
who has struggled along with me through the same general
procedure at week-end painting, has perfected his still-life
technique to a high degree. I have never tried to do still life,
but someday I may break down and have a go at it.

After you have developed considerable painting skill, you
may try a portrait of yourself. It's done with the aid of a big
mirror.

The subject matter for pictures, like the subject matter for
fiction, is limitless.

❀　❀

Sometimes a person will walk by when you are painting—a
person that would be a suitable figure for your picture if he or
she would stand still or come by later at a time when you were
ready to put in a figure. One way in which I have solved this
problem is to sketch the figure in colors on a clean place on my
palette and later work with the sketch as my study or notebook.
The drawing has to be done on the fly, but it is good practice.

❀　❀

At the New York World's Fair in 1939, the exhibition of Old Masters commanded a great deal of my attention. On close examination of one of the more modern Masters I discovered that he had shared one of my own problems. There were several bristles from his brushes in the paint on his canvas. Turning to several strangers near by, I could not refrain from commenting on this discovery. With considerable hauteur, one of them sneered, "I suppose it makes you very happy to find broken bristles in somebody's picture!"

❋ ❋

To loosen the top of a stuck tube of paint, use either pliers or a small flame. Pliers are usually the easier. Incidentally, the flame does not expand the cap to effect the loosening; it merely softens the dried paint so that the cap can be unscrewed.

If you have not painted for a long time, make sure that all your tube caps are loosened before you leave home on a sketching trip. It's much easier to check them then than to try to unscrew them later.

❋ ❋

It does not often pay to paint a new picture over an old one. It is difficult to draw over strong colors; nor is it economical to reuse an old canvas, because it takes more paint to cover a picture than it does to cover a clean canvas. Panels are cheaper than paint.

❋ ❋

Sometimes a tube of color breaks, and the paint starts to leak out or dry up. It can be saved by squeezing it all out into a clean, very small ointment jar purchased from the drugstore.

❋ ❋

If there is much unused tube color on your palette when you are ending a day's work and packing up to go home, it is a good plan to settle it down in low mounds by striking the underside of the palette with the palm of your hand directly beneath the color. If the unused paint stands up too high, it may touch the picture when your box is closed and ruin the work of hours, or the color may slide down and make a mess when the box is being carried by the handle.

❋   ❋

When time is short for outdoor work, it is possible to save a few minutes by laying the palette before going out. But it is important that the colors be jarred down so that they do not slip down the palette when you are en route to or from your painting place.

❋   ❋

While I do not expect the Week-end Painter to sell many of his pictures, I cannot refrain from commenting on the economics of art. The purpose of art is to arouse an emotion in the beholder. This is accomplished by emphasis, even exaggeration, in the portrayal of the theme. People will seldom pay out good money for art that does not arouse pleasant emotions. If a picture repels and disgusts, the market for that picture is limited to a few persons who are attracted to grotesqueries, abnormalities, and morbid subjects.

If I understand the term "sincerity" as applied to art, I do not believe that an artist is necessarily insincere in his work just because he uses common horse sense and chooses pleasant subject matters for his pictures.

❋   ❋

The same principles of color and composition apply to water-color painting as to oil painting. Only the techniques differ.

❋   ❋

Still life can afford you with plenty of subject matter when
for some reason you do not wish to venture outside. The still
life has certain advantages over the landscape: the objects can
be arranged in any composition you desire and kept that way
as long as you want. If you expose your still life to a north light,
the problem caused by the changing of the sun's position will
be avoided.

*   *

Flower pictures are a real test of an artist's skill. But they
must be done with a certain degree of speed, for flowers fade
and droop in a few days. The principal fascination of flower
painting is the great variety of Hues, Values, and Chromas to
be found in a mixed bouquet. It affords one an opportunity to
paint with colors that have very little other use. But it imposes
on the artist an obligation to arrange the flowers in a good
composition—something that is easier said than done.

*   *

Your own pictures will often make acceptable Christmas or
other gifts, especially to members of your family or relatives.
I should counsel, however, that you be a little cautious about
thrusting your early attempts on others. Be reasonably sure
that a picture is really one that the recipient will be proud of,
not one that he will display only because of loyalty.

*   *

As you progress in your painting you will want to buy the
pictures of professional artists. It is astonishing to learn how
few people have any idea of the value of pictures, too many
being of the opinion that an oil painting is *per se* a thing of
tremendous value simply because it is an oil painting. On one
occasion I made a study of the prices and sizes of pictures at an
exhibition of well-known contemporary American artists, most

of whom were good craftsmen. Except for a very few pictures, which for some unrevealed reason were most expensive, the bulk of the canvases at the exhibit were priced at figures very close to 50 cents a square inch. Whenever I have mentioned this crude rule-of-thumb method of estimating the cost of good contemporary American works, my ideas have been greeted with derision. Yet I believe that, except for the paintings of a few of our most accomplished artists, this figure is not far wrong, and certainly it would be no insult to any professional artist to offer him such a figure.

Things are not very different in England. At the Royal Academy exhibition in London, in May, 1945, I carried a slide rule, divided the selling price of fifteen pictures by their area, and found that the prices were only somewhat higher than those in the United States. Figuring the British pound at par, the average price per square inch was 88 cents, the lowest price among the pictures I noted was 35 cents a square inch, while the highest was $2.69, with more than half the pictures falling into the average-figure category. To form this estimate, I took paintings serially as they came and did not pick out any special ones for careful study. It should be noted, too, that these British pictures were selling like hot cakes.

Of course, you would not begin a conversation with an artist by asking how much per square inch his work was worth, but it would be a fair basis for estimating the probable price of a new picture. After that what you paid would be a matter of negotiation.

*　*

Occasionally I purchase a picture, despite the fact that my closet is full of my own paintings. I find that it is often helpful to ask the artist to aid me in selecting something that he regards as typical of his work—the sort of picture he would like to be remembered by. Of course, if the suggested picture does not please me, I do not buy it. But often you can pick up some particularly good specimens of an artist's work in this manner.

*   *

It is a good plan to date all your pictures when you paint them. After a few years have elapsed it is difficult to recall the year in which you did any particular job.

Progress in painting is not a slow and steady ascent up a straight incline toward perfection. On the contrary, it is a stepwise phenomenon. For a long time you will work on a low plane of quality, and then unexpectedly you will discover some new trick of the craft and will realize that you have ascended to a higher plateau of painting ability. Life contributes few moments of greater exhilaration than these when you realize you have achieved a higher level of quality in your painting.

The important thing is not to be discouraged when you remain on a single plane of performance for several months. How quickly you can get to a higher plane is determined largely by your own attitude. If you experiment, you will one day discover a better way. If you do not experiment, your progress and escape from mediocrity will be much slower.

Sometimes it is a good thing to get out your dated pictures and arrange them in chronological order around a room. Don't hang them, but stand them against the wall. You can then determine whether or not you have been making progress. But always remember that progress upward is not a smoothly flowing adventure. One day you are on one level. The next day you are on a much higher level, and often you will not know how you got there.

*   *

For years I tried to find my way about in the manner of the French Impressionists, but nothing I attempted would "jell."

If I had wanted to *copy* a Claude Monet or a Sisley, it would have been a simple matter to go to a museum and attempt to do so. What I really wanted to know, however, was *how* they did their work in the technique they developed in the latter years of the nineteenth century. After at least twenty tries, I arrived at the conclusion that the Impressionistic manner had some very definite limitations and that I was trying to make it do too much. Instead of the smooth charm of a Sisley land-scape, I was eternally producing pictures whose chief character-istic could only be classified as "smallpox." My attempts were merely spotty and lacked any semblance of the broken color I wanted to achieve. What could be wrong?

Every time I went to Washington I would spend an hour in the Chester Dale Collection in the National Gallery where there are some excellent examples of the work of the Impres-sionists, and after several years of sporadic observation it dawned on me that Impressionism omits vigorous contrasts of lights and darks and that I had been attempting to include something the Impressionists had, perforce, left out. Business cares have never permitted me to make the detailed studies necessary to reduce my observations to a quantitative basis, but, if you will realize that the following comment is a mere "guesstimate," I will say that the maximum apparent contrast between lights and darks in a good Impressionist picture is not more than 4 points on the Value scale. In other words, such a picture seems to be painted between 4 Value and 8 Value. In contrast, I was trying to stretch out my Value dispersion from 1 to 9, which accounts for the unpleasant spottiness of my work—what might justly have been called its approximation to smallpox.

Just about the time I reached this conclusion I chanced to discuss the problem with a professional artist. He suggested I read Birge Harrison's *Landscape Painting*. It seems that Mr.

Harrison knew all about my discovery some forty years ago, for here is what he says: "The value of the overtone must in every case exactly match the value of the undertone. While we wish to secure broken color, we *must avoid broken Values*, for they utterly destroy atmosphere."

This convinced me. Broken Values were creating the unpleasant spotted condition of my work, and henceforth I modified my style.

❋ ❋

Speaking of the omission of trivial details in a painting, Birge Harrison also said, "A picture is often completed long before you suspect it."

❋ ❋

And, again quoting Birge Harrison, "Prepare for refraction as they [the French Impressionists] did, by lowering Values as you approach the edge so that the final stroke which draws your limb or your tree may be as fresh and as crisp as possible without being hard; and, if you are painting in broken color, then do all this preparatory work fully and carefully in the undertone, so that the final painting may be accomplished with that dash and freedom which, say what you may, will always remain an admirable quality in a picture."

NINETEEN

Books I Have Read

ON SEVERAL occasions I have indicated that many books have been written about painting and about pictures. To such books I probably owe much of my so-called "self-instruction," certainly as much as I owe to talking with artists or looking at their finished works. Because it is difficult to recall the source of any particular bit of technique, I am listing all the art books in my personal library. If I have unconsciously quoted any ideas without proper credit, it is due to my own faulty memory.

I would not recommend to every beginner that he buy every one of these books. They represent quite a bit of money. Some are about appreciation of art; some are biographical; some are strictly scientific; some are decidedly technical and discuss the "how to" of painting; and some are almost entirely pictorial, having either black-and-white reproductions or colored ones or both.

Unfortunately, I do not own all the good books about painting. The omission of certain recently published volumes from my list has no significance other than their absence from my library. And some good older books on painting never came to my attention until this list was ready for the printer.

Anyone who is struggling along without an instructor needs to study many paintings to see how the other fellow has solved his problems. If there is a large museum handy, that can be decidedly helpful. But if, like myself, you have to travel a considerable distance to a museum of art, then a collection of books of color reproductions is a fairly good substitute. This is

the excuse I give my wife for having so many art books in my library.

Black-and-white reproductions, though far from satisfying, are useful to teach what Values an artist has used, what subjects, and how he has composed them. Good color reproductions are more desirable.

A few of these volumes I have really studied; some I have scanned once and set aside. In studying art books I have not been seeking a cultural education in art but have been trying to learn craftsmanship—how to paint. The comments that accompany the name of each book in the list give my own opinion of its value judged from this viewpoint.

You cannot study the craftsmanship of art without simultaneously acquiring considerable cultural knowledge. But, alas, the books that deal with appreciation and culture seldom give the reader anything on the techniques employed by the artist. To acquire information about techniques you must study the artists' actual works. And no better method of study has come to my aid than the copying of good pictures. Several copies that I have done from reproductions of Van Gogh or De Vlaminck have taught me more about technical methods than all the readings and conversations of a decade.

As I have indicated previously, I paint pictures for fun, to please myself and—I hope—my wife, who generously tolerates them around the house. Occasionally I have been credited—unjustly, I fear—with introducing a quality of spirituality into my painting. I can assure you, however, that any such spirituality has been purely accidental. It seems to be associated with a tackiness of surface that comes when I work over a picture on the second day and the paint is not quite dry. The effect is pleasing to me, and I let it remain. Possibly some of the methods of the great artists of the past have been the result of just such fortuitous discoveries. Yet, if writers and critics grow ec-

static about them in esoteric and mystical phraseology without knowing how the effect was produced, the reader who wants to learn the know-how will hardly profit.

Hence, if I dismiss a book as merely cultural, it is not a condemnation of the book for the purpose its author had in mind when he produced it; it is solely that I have felt that its utility to me as an aid in developing craftsmanship has been limited.

Here then, is my library:

TECHNICAL

ANONYMOUS: Three Monographs on Color:
    I. *Color Chemistry*
   II. *Color as Light*
  III. *Color in Use*
The research laboratories of The International Printing Ink Corporation, New York.

Very technical on color. While written for designers, I find these three small volumes fine aids to understanding Hue, Value, and Chroma as developed by Albert H. Munsell. Worth studying—if you can get them.

BIRREN, Faber: *Color Dimensions*. The Crimson Press, Chicago.

Very technical. Color from the viewpoint of psychology. More useful to designers than to artists. Interesting, but I prefer the Munsell System myself.

BURROUGHS, Alan: *Art Criticism from a Laboratory*. Little, Brown & Company, Boston.

Criticism of Old Masters with the aid of the X ray.

COMPANA, D. M.: *Teacher of Picture-frames Finishing*. Maurer-Compana Art Company, Chicago.

A booklet I have never used.

CARLSON, John F.: *Elementary Principles of Landscape Painting*. Published by the author, Woodstock, N.Y.

Worth owning, but only the chapter on "Pure Mechanicalities" is particularly helpful to one who has no teacher.

DAVIDSON, Morris: *Painting for Pleasure*. Hale, Cushman & Flint, Inc., Boston.

Presumably for the beginner but omits much that is needed by the self-taught artist.

GETTENS and STOUT: *Painting Materials*. D. Van Nostrand Company, Inc., New York.

Technical on materials—not on methods of painting.

HILL, Adrian: *On Drawing and Painting Trees*. Sir Isaac Pitman & Sons, Ltd., London.

Worth studying for the beginner, but the overconscientious author stops short of telling how to paint a tree lest the student acquire his methods.

KEEL-SMITH, Hilda: *My Drawing Book: Self-instruction Drawing, Step Four*. Rand McNally & Company, Chicago.

A kid's book, given me as a joke. I found it helped me learn perspective drawing.

LOOMIS, Andrew: *Figure Drawing for All It's Worth*. The Viking Press, Inc., New York.

On drawing figures.

LORAN, Erle: *Cézanne's Composition*. University of California Press, Berkeley, Calif.

Very technical. For advanced students of composition. Yet it is very useful even for a beginner because it shows actual photographs of the scenes from which Cézanne painted his landscapes alongside black-and-white reproductions of the paintings inspired by the scenes.

Lutz, E. G.: *Practical Landscape Painting in Oils.* Charles Scribner's Sons, New York.

Useful for beginners. All illustrations in black and white.

Martini, Herbert E.: *Color.* Bridgman Publishers, Pelham, New York.

Technical on color. For the artist. Tends to reduce painting to a formula rather than an experiment.

Mayer, Ralph: *The Artist's Handbook of Materials and Techniques.* The Viking Press, Inc., New York.

Technical but does not tell how to paint.

Newberry, Clare Turlay: *Drawing a Cat.* The Studio Publications, Inc., London.

O'Hara, Eliot: *Making the Brush Behave (More about Watercolor).* Minton, Balch & Co., New York.

Helpful for beginners in water color.

O'Hara, Eliot: *Making Watercolor Behave.* Minton, Balch & Co., New York.

Helpful for beginners in water color. His later writings do not always quite agree with his advice here.

Perard, Victor: *Anatomy and Drawing.* Published by the author, New York.

Human-figure drawings.

Perard, Victor: *Hands and Their Construction.* Pitman Publishing Corp., New York.

On drawing hands.

RICHMOND, L., and J. LITTLEJOHNS: *The Technique of Water-color Painting*. Pitman Publishing Corp., New York.

Interesting but has not been particularly helpful to me. It is a companion to another work of theirs on oil painting which I do not own.

RINES, Frank M.: *Design and Construction in Tree Drawing*. Bridgman Publishers, Inc., Pelham, N.Y.

Strictly technical and helpful.

ZAIDENBERG, Arthur: *Anyone Can Draw*. Illustrated Editions Co., Inc., New York.

Mostly about the human form divine but about drawing nevertheless.

ZAIDENBERG, Arthur: *Anyone Can Paint*. Crown Publishers, New York.

More about drawing than painting but worth study. However, it leaves off where the unaided need help.

CULTURAL AND BIOGRAPHICAL

ANDERSON, John J., Jr.: *The Unknown Turner*. Privately printed for the author, New York.

Biographical and cultural. Black-and-white reproductions and colored frontispiece.

ANONYMOUS: *American Painting Today*, with an essay by Forbes Watson. The American Federation of Arts, Washington, D.C.

Cultural, with many black-and-white and colored reproductions.

ANONYMOUS: *Museum of Modern Western Art in Moscow*. State Publishers, "Art," Moscow.

A collection of colored reproductions, principally of work by the French Impressionists, many of which are very stimulating.

BARR, Alfred H., Jr.: *Vincent Van Gogh*. The Museum of Modern Art, New York.

Biographical, with black-and-white reproductions.

BERTRAM, Anthony: *The World's Masters—Claude Monet*. William E. Rudge's Sons, Inc., Varick, N.Y.

Theory of Impressionism, with black-and-white reproductions from Monet.

BOSWELL, Peyton, Jr.: *George Bellows*. Crown Publishers, New York.

Biographical, with colored and half-tone reproductions.

BOSWELL, Peyton, Jr.: *Modern American Painting*. Dodd, Mead & Company, Inc., New York.

Cultural, with many color reproductions.

BOSWELL, Peyton, Jr.: *Varnum Poor*. Hyperion Press of New York, Inc., New York.

Biographical, with half tones and colored reproductions.

CRANE, Aimée, and Edward Alden JEWELL: *French Impressionists*. Hyperion Press of New York, Inc., New York.

Black-and-white and colored reproductions. Worth study.

CRAVEN, Thomas: *A Treasury of Art Masterpieces*. Simon and Schuster, Inc., New York.

Color reproductions.

DURET, Theodore: *Manet*. Crown Publishers, New York.

Biographical, with colored and half-tone reproductions.

DURET, Theodore: *Renoir*. Crown Publishers, New York.

Biographical, with color and half-tone reproductions.

GLÜCK, Gustav: *Pieter Brueghel the Elder*. Editions Hyperion, Paris.

Cultural, with half-tone and color reproductions.

GOODRICH, Lloyd: *Winslow Homer*. The Macmillan Company, New York.

Biographical. No color reproductions but plenty of half tones.

HENRI, Robert: *The Art Spirit*. J. B. Lippincott Company, Philadelphia.

A bit heavy on the spiritual side of art but has many suggestions about craftsmanship that are worth reading. In particular I like these: "No knowledge is so easily found as when it is needed." "It is easier, I think, to paint a good picture than it is to paint a bad one."

ISHAM, Samuel: *The History of American Painting*. The Macmillan Company, New York.

Cultural, with half tones.

JEWELL, Edward Alden: *Paul Cézanne*. Hyperion Press of New York, Inc., New York.

Cultural biography. Many reproductions in half tone and color.

LAFARGUE, Marc: *Corot*. John Lane, The Bodley Head, Ltd., London.

Cultural biography, with half-tone illustrations.

LASSAIGNE, Jacques: *Daumier*. French & European Publications, Inc., New York.

Colored and half-tone reproductions, largely of human figures.

MACK, Gerstle: *Toulouse-Lautrec*. Alfred A. Knopf, Inc., New York.

Biographical.

NICHOLS, H. S.: *Fifty Drawings by Aubrey Beardsley*. H. S. Nichols, New York.

PACH, Walter: *Queer Thing, Painting*. Harper & Brothers, New York.

Cultural.

PACH, Walter: *Vincent Van Gogh*. The Art Book Publications, Inc., New York.

Cultural and biographical, with a few colored and half-tone reproductions.

PERLS, Klaus: *Vlaminck*. Hyperion Press of New York, Inc., New York.

Biographical, with colored and black-and-white reproductions.

PIRIE, J. Greig: *World Famous Paintings*. W. & G. Foyle, Ltd., London.

Color reproductions.

RAZOUMOVSKAJA, S.: *Corot in the Museums of the U.S.S.R.* Puskin Museum of Fine Arts. Moscow.

Reproduction in color of some of Corot's paintings owned in Russia. A few are worth while.

REWALD, John: *Georges Seurat*. Wittenborn and Co., New York.

Biographical, with a disappointingly brief description of Seurat's principles and techniques. Half-tone illustrations—no color.

REWALD, John: *Malliol.* Hyperion Press of New York, Inc., New York.

Sculpture.

ROURKE, Constance: *Charles Sheeler, Artist in the American Tradition.* Harcourt, Brace & Company, Inc., New York.

Cultural. Half-tone reproductions.

SAINT-GAUDENS, Homer: *The American Artist and His Times.* Dodd, Mead & Company, New York.

Cultural. Half-tone reproductions.

SCHILD, Constance: *The Complete Etchings of Rembrandt.* Arden Book Company, New York.

Reproductions of etchings.

STONE, Irving: *Lust for Life, A Novel about Vincent Van Gogh.* The Heritage Press, New York.

Half-tone illustrations. A good yarn, probably a bit exaggerated in spots. Worth reading if you are discouraged by slow progress.

TERRASSE, Charles: *French Paintings in the Twentieth Century.* Editions Hyperion, Paris.

Half tones and colored reproductions.

VAN DYKE, John C.: *Rembrandt and His School.* Charles Scribner's Sons, New York.

A critique of pictures attributed to Rembrandt. Black-and-white reproductions.

VAN LOON, Hendrick Willem: *The Arts.* Simon and Schuster, Inc., New York.

Cultural.

VARGA, Margit: *Waldo Peirce*. Hyperion Press of New York, Inc., New York.

Biographical, with colored and half-tone reproductions.

VAUGHN, Malcolm: *Derain*. Hyperion Press of New York, Inc., New York.

Biographical, with colored and half-tone reproductions.

VOLLARD, Ambroise: *Paul Cézanne, His Life and Art*. Crown Publishers, New York.

Entertaining biography. Colored and half-tone reproductions.

VOLLARD, Ambroise: *Recollections of a Picture Dealer*. Little, Brown & Company, Boston.

Cultural and commercial; highly entertaining reading.

WATSON, Forbes: *Winslow Homer*. Crown Publishers, New York.

Biographical. Half-tone reproductions.

WILENSKI, R. H.: *Modern French Painters*. Reynal & Hitchcock, Inc., New York.

Contains only black-and-white reproductions. A vast text on the cultural aspects of French Moderns.

I must not conclude the list of the printed helps to the self taught artist without mentioning the periodicals *American Artist* published in New York and *The Artist* published in London.

The Artist is more frankly slanted at the beginner than *American Artist* but you will derive more benefit from the latter because it is written in the American idiom rather than the British idiom. If you embark on painting as a hobby you should read it regularly.

Index

A

B